Positive Words

Adult Coloring Book

By Mary Ellen Lee

Publishing services provided by:

Archangel Ink

ISBN: 1-942761-75-9

ISBN-13: 978-1-942761-75-4

Contents

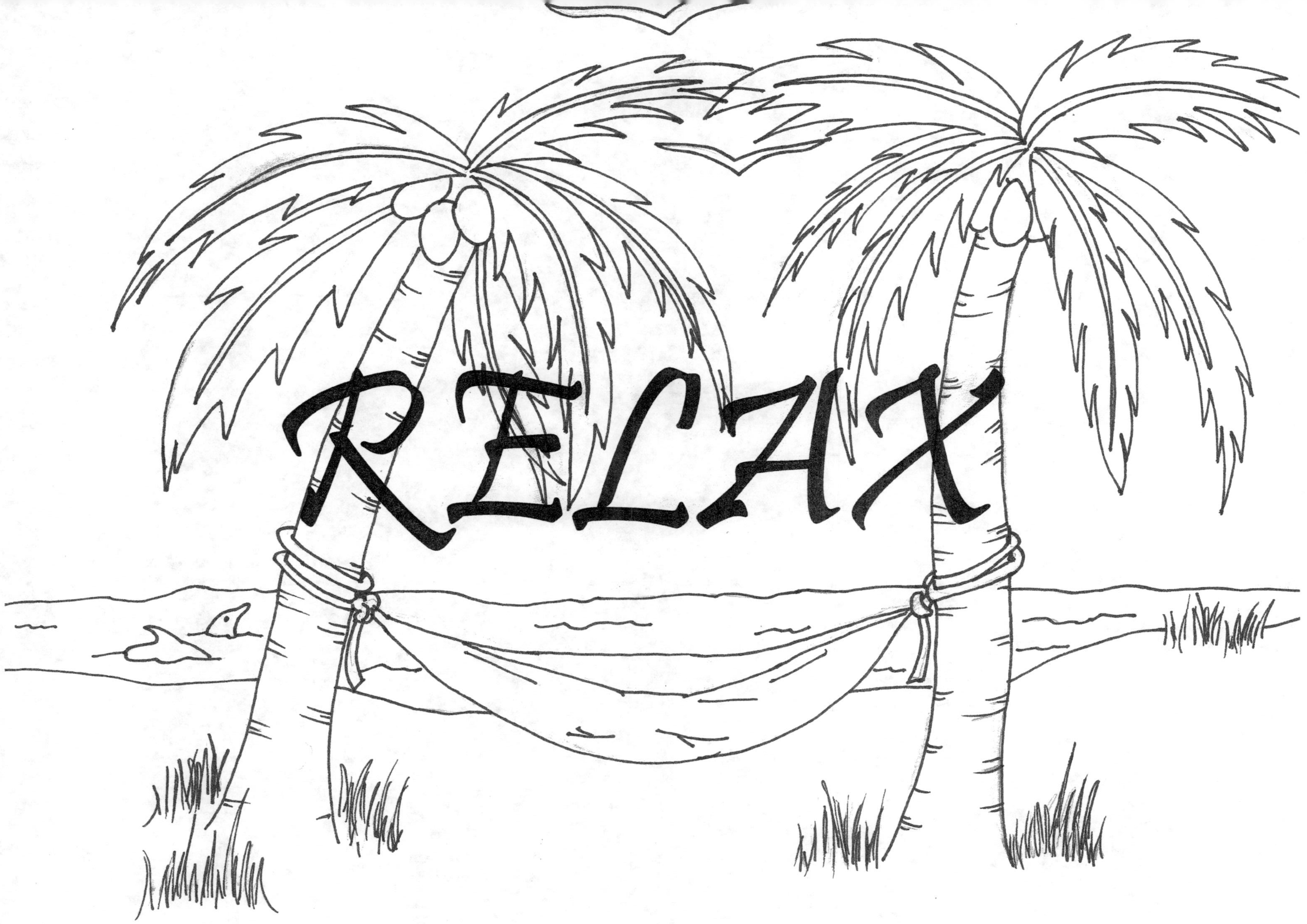
RELAX

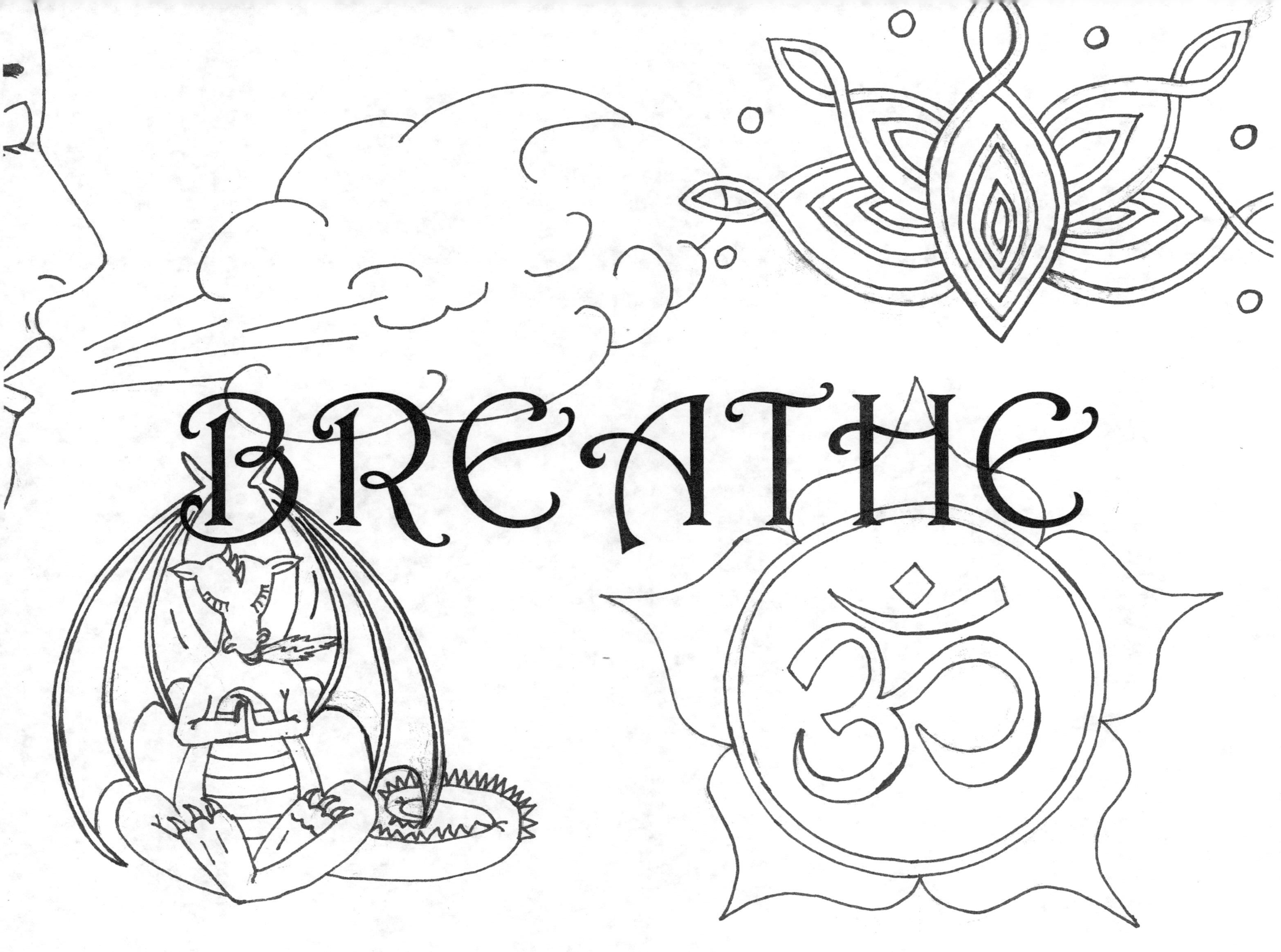
BREATHE

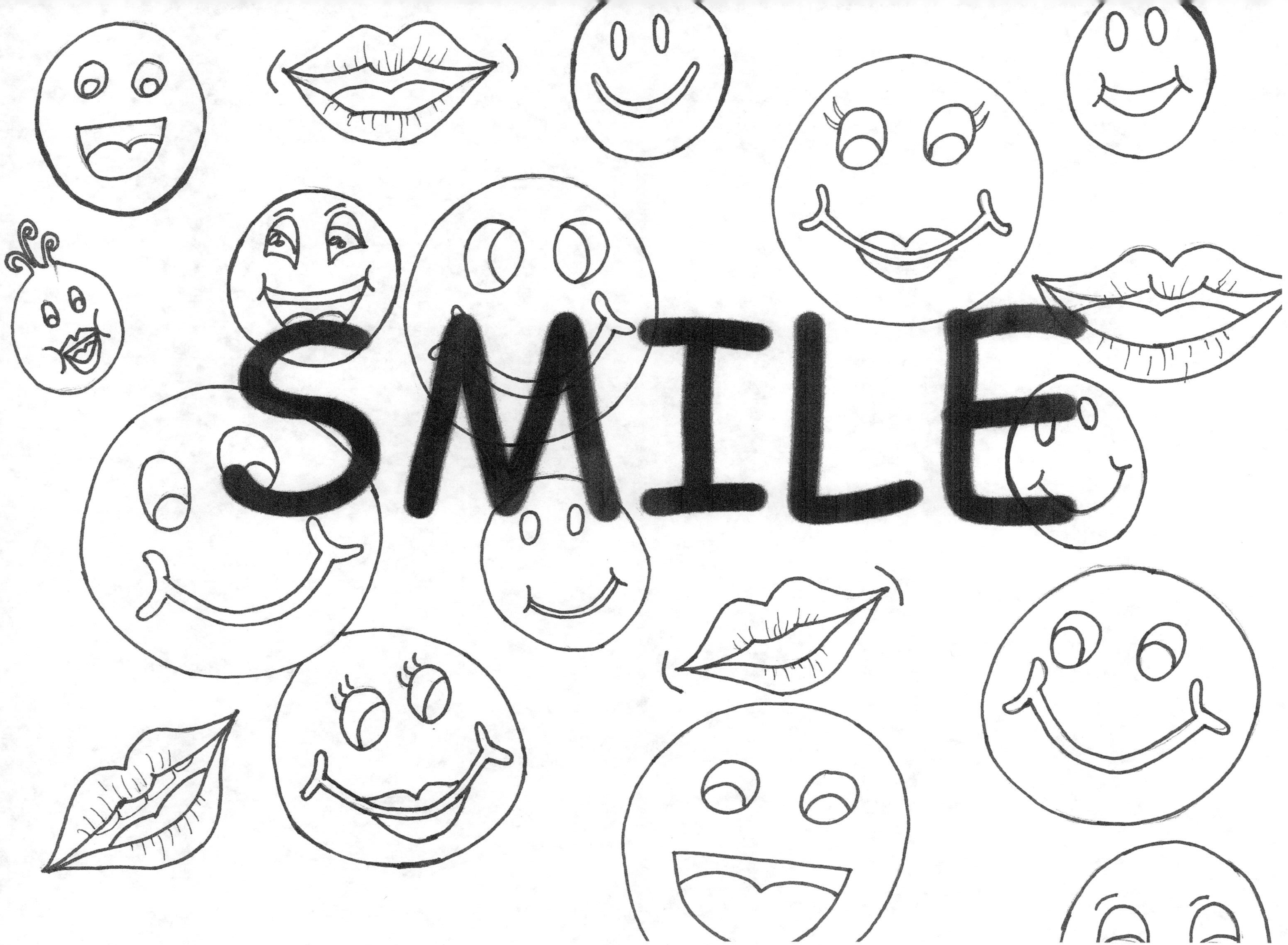
SMILE

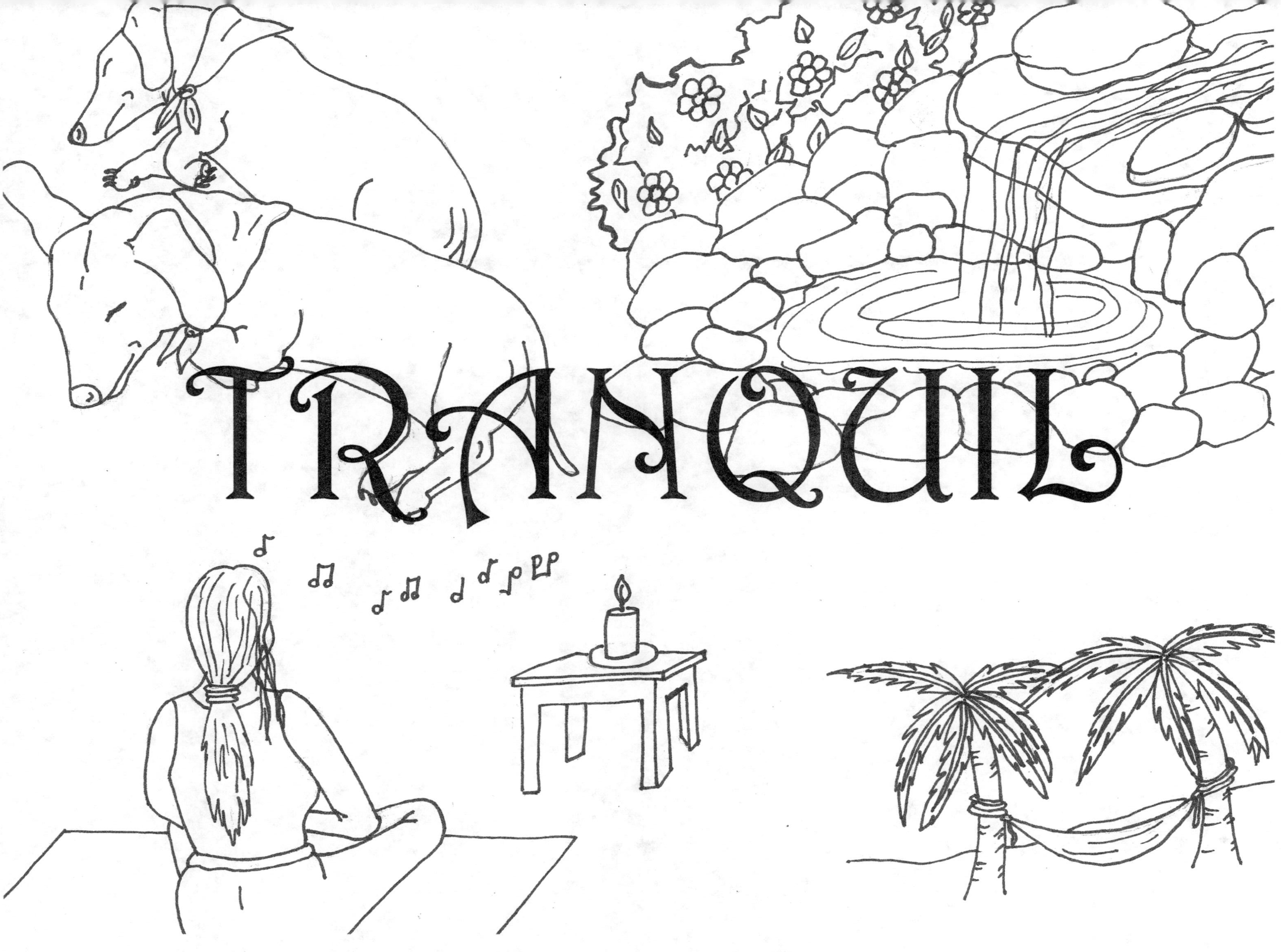
TRANQUIL

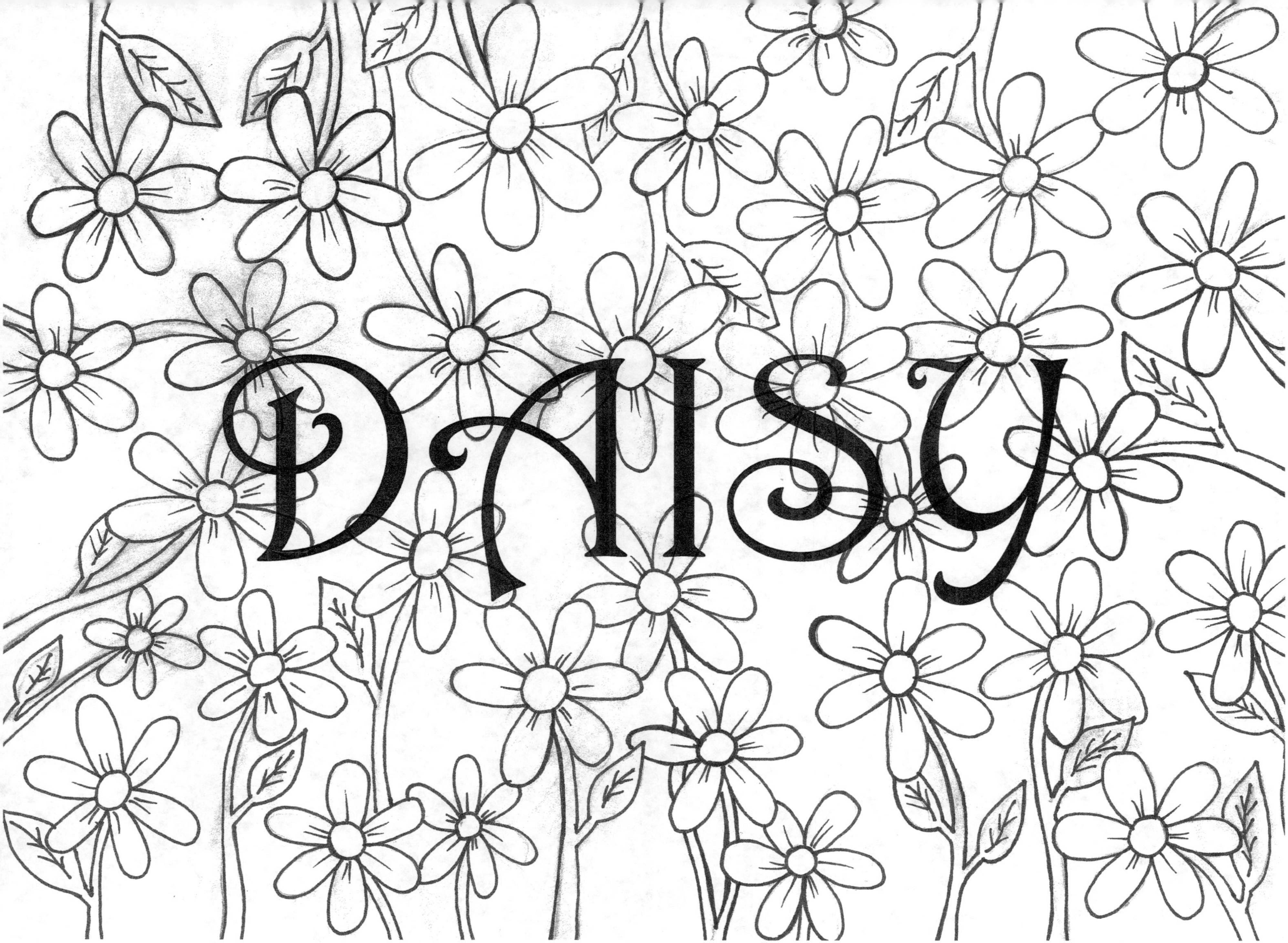
DAISY

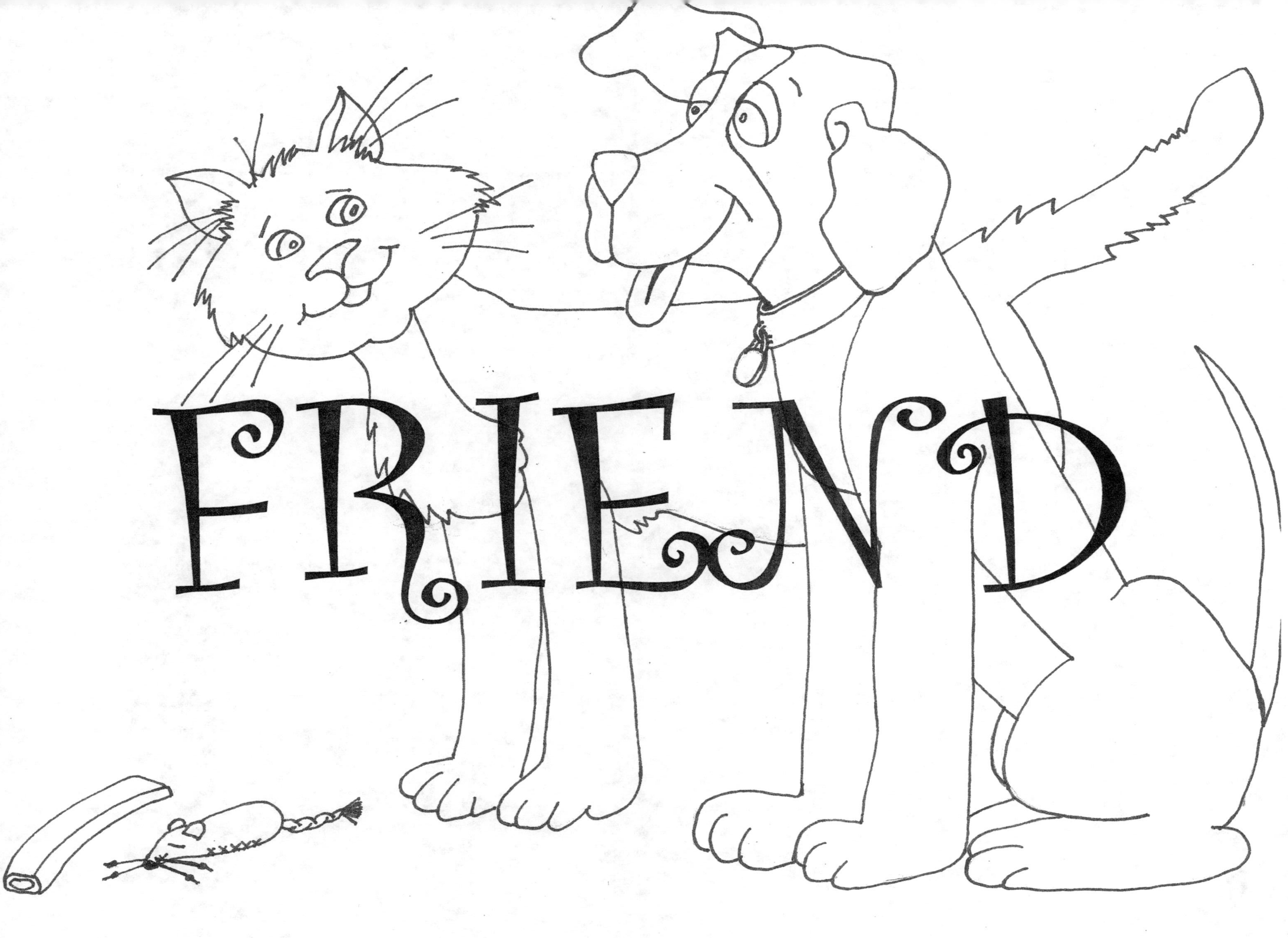
FRIEND

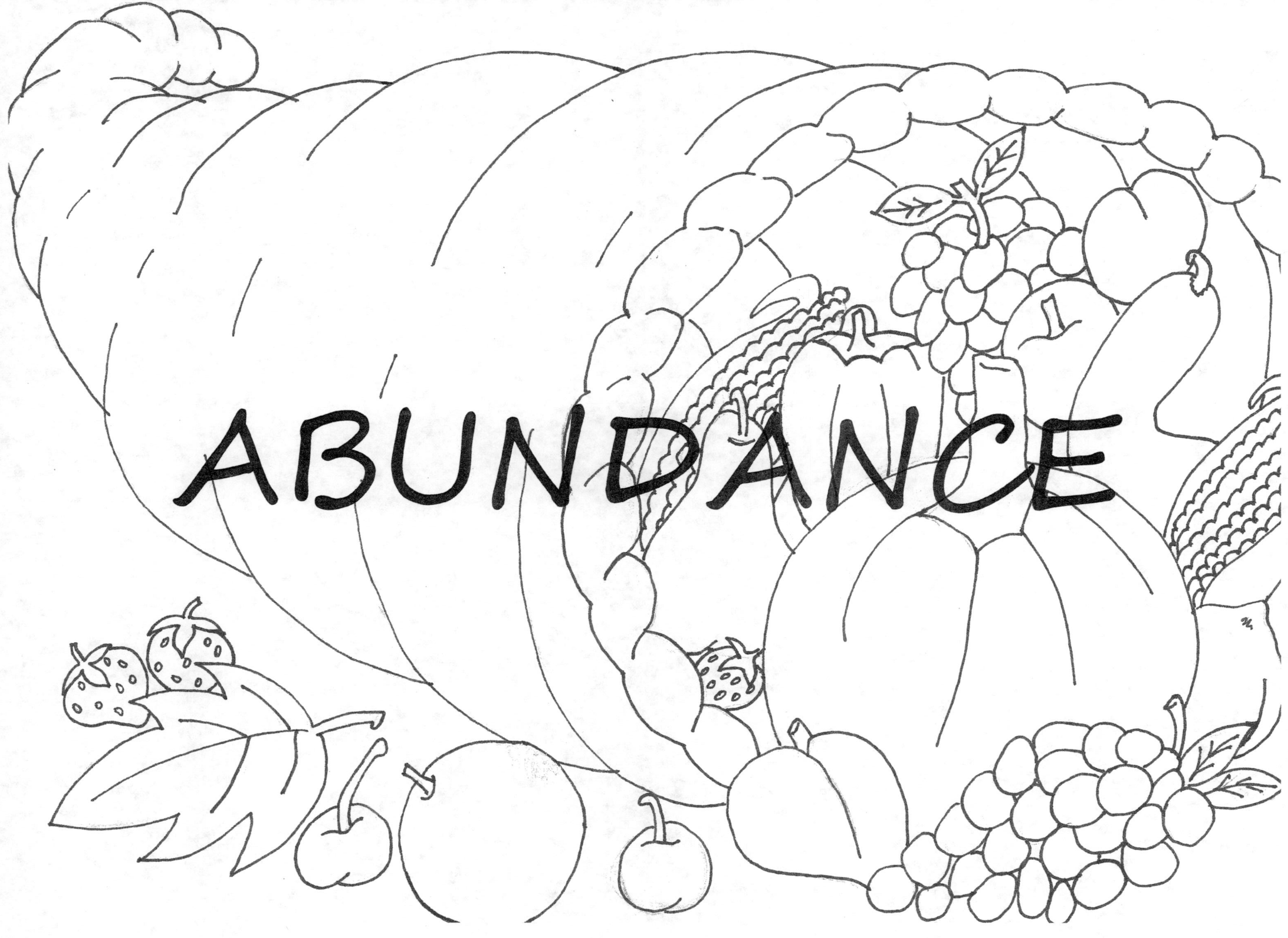
ABUNDANCE

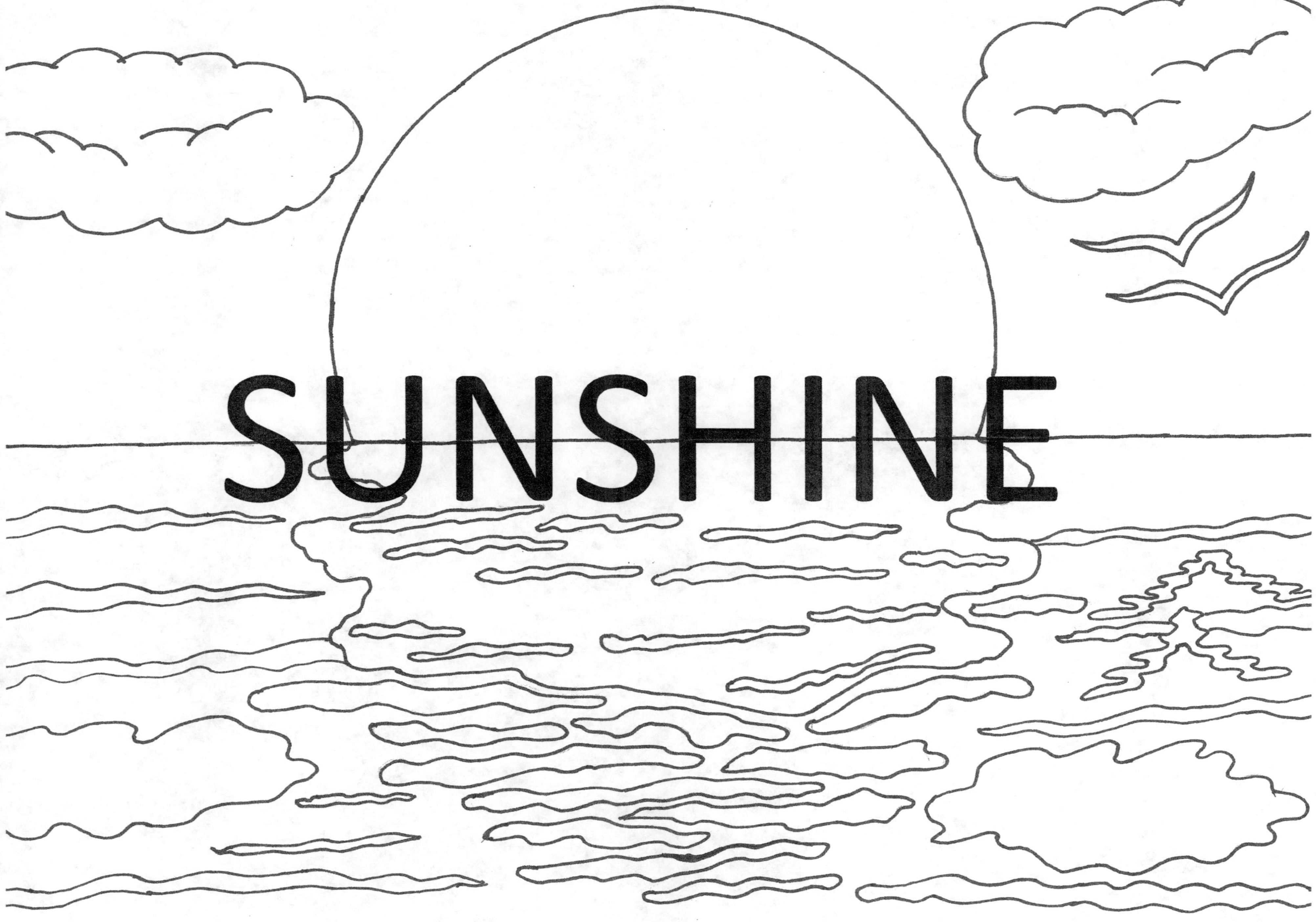
SUNSHINE

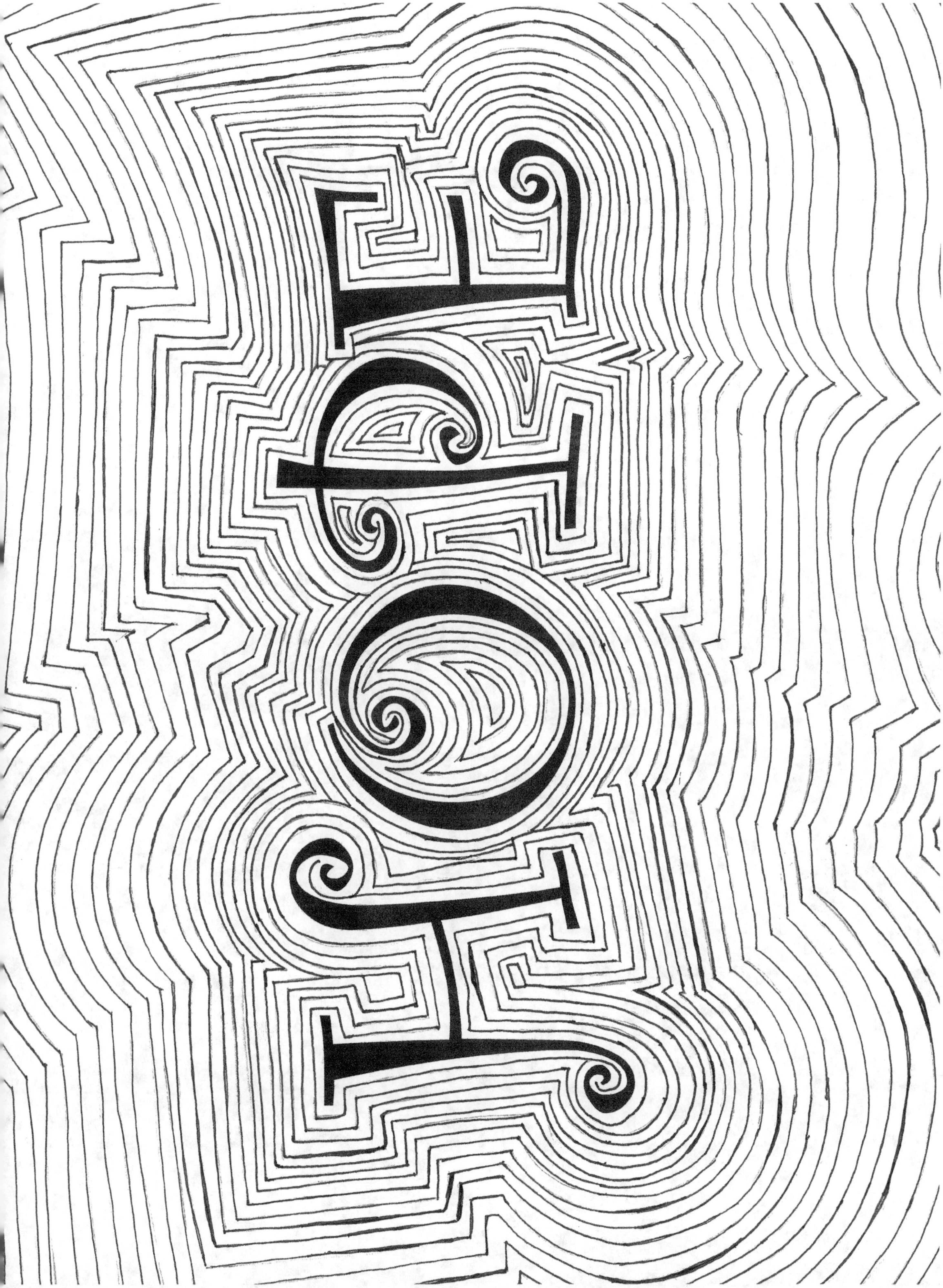
HOPE

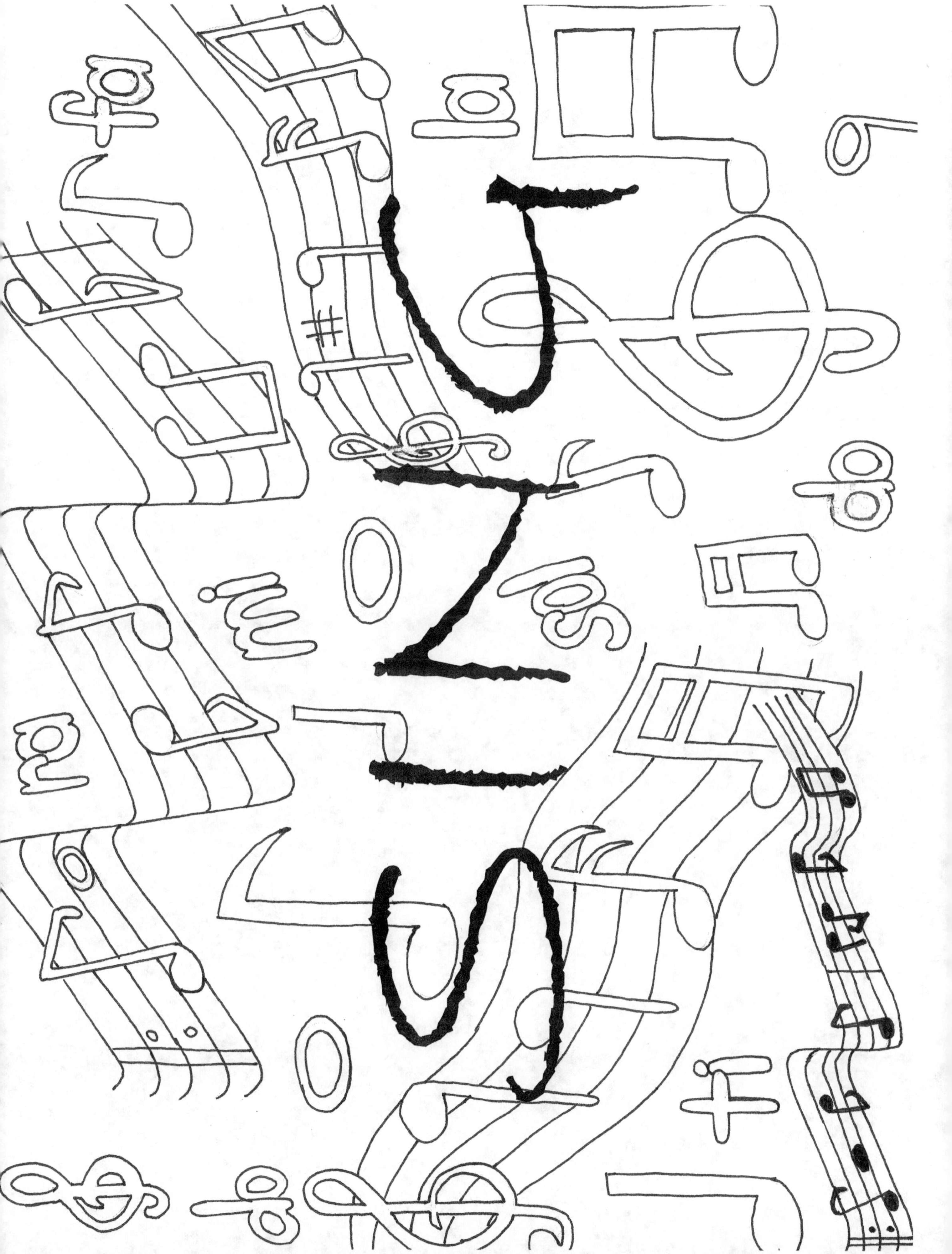

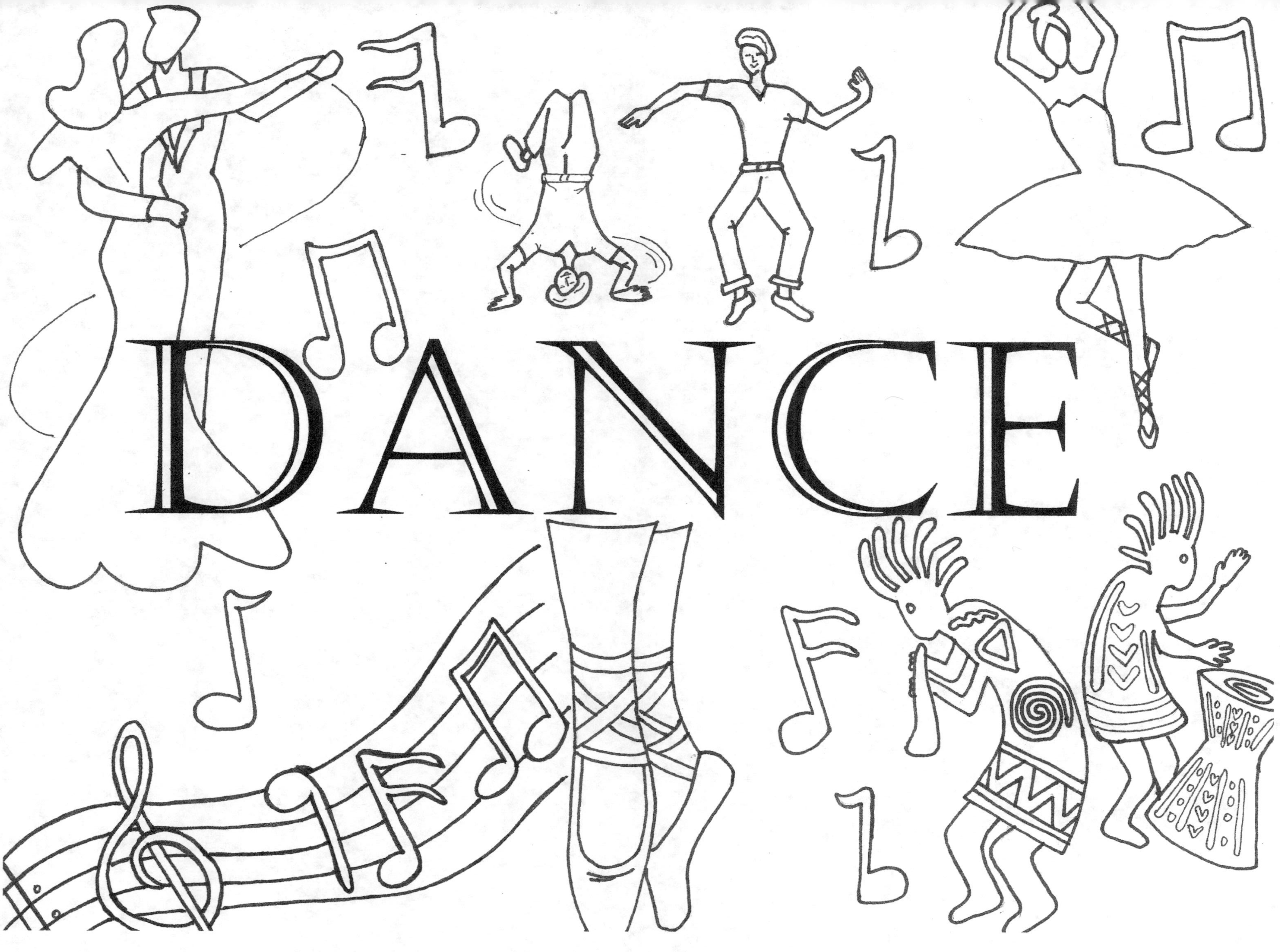
DANCE

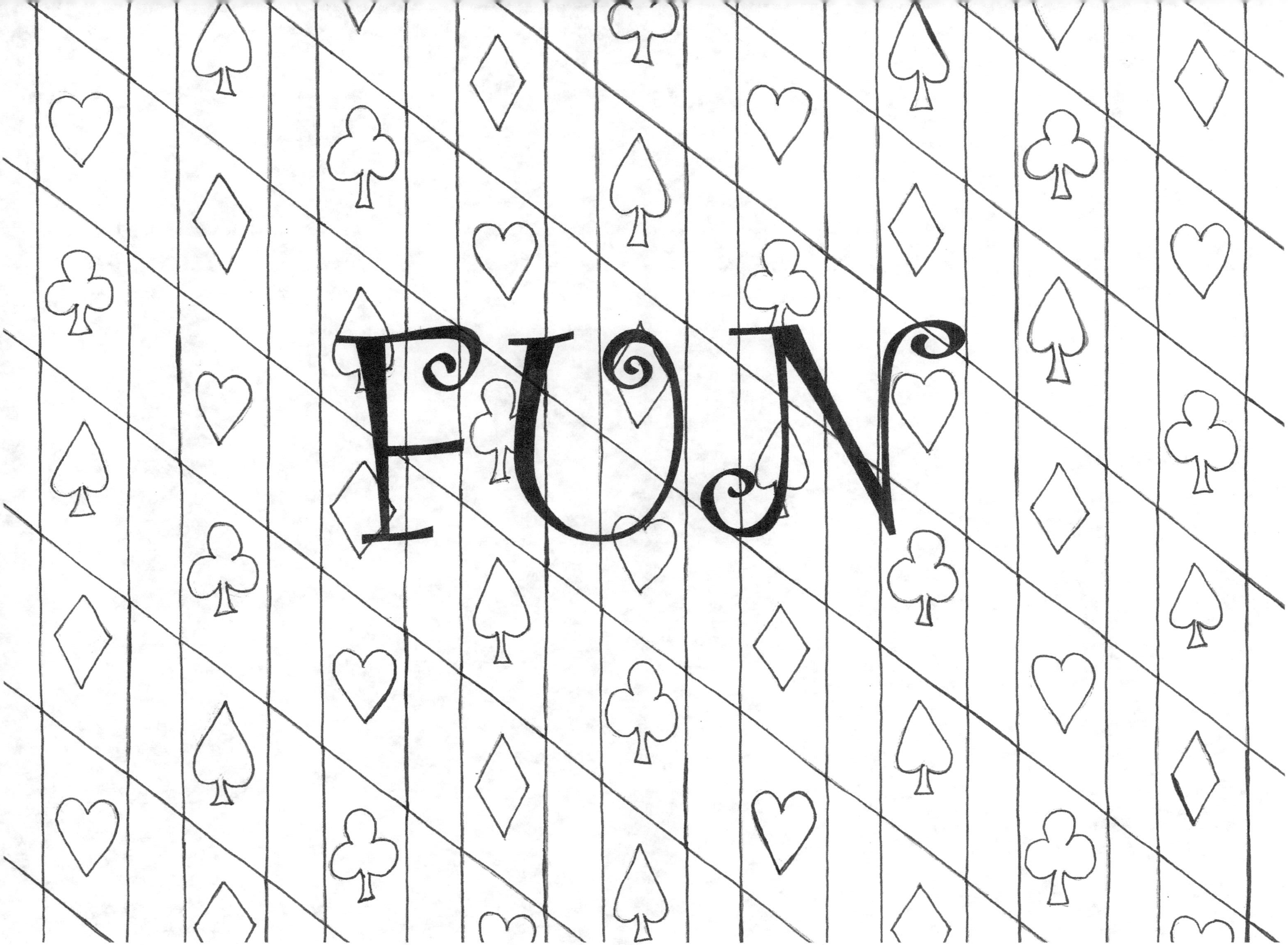
FUN

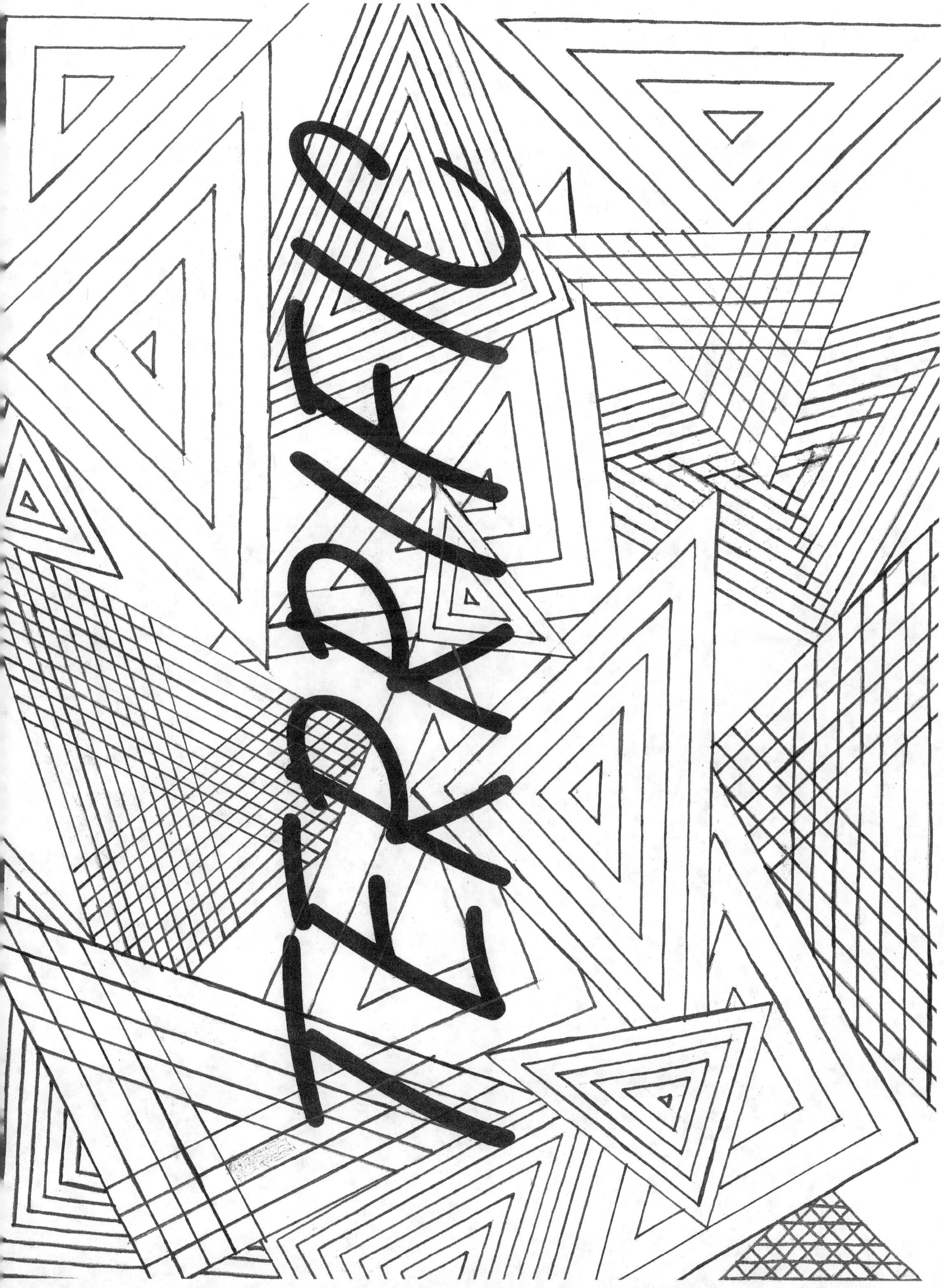
TERRIFIC

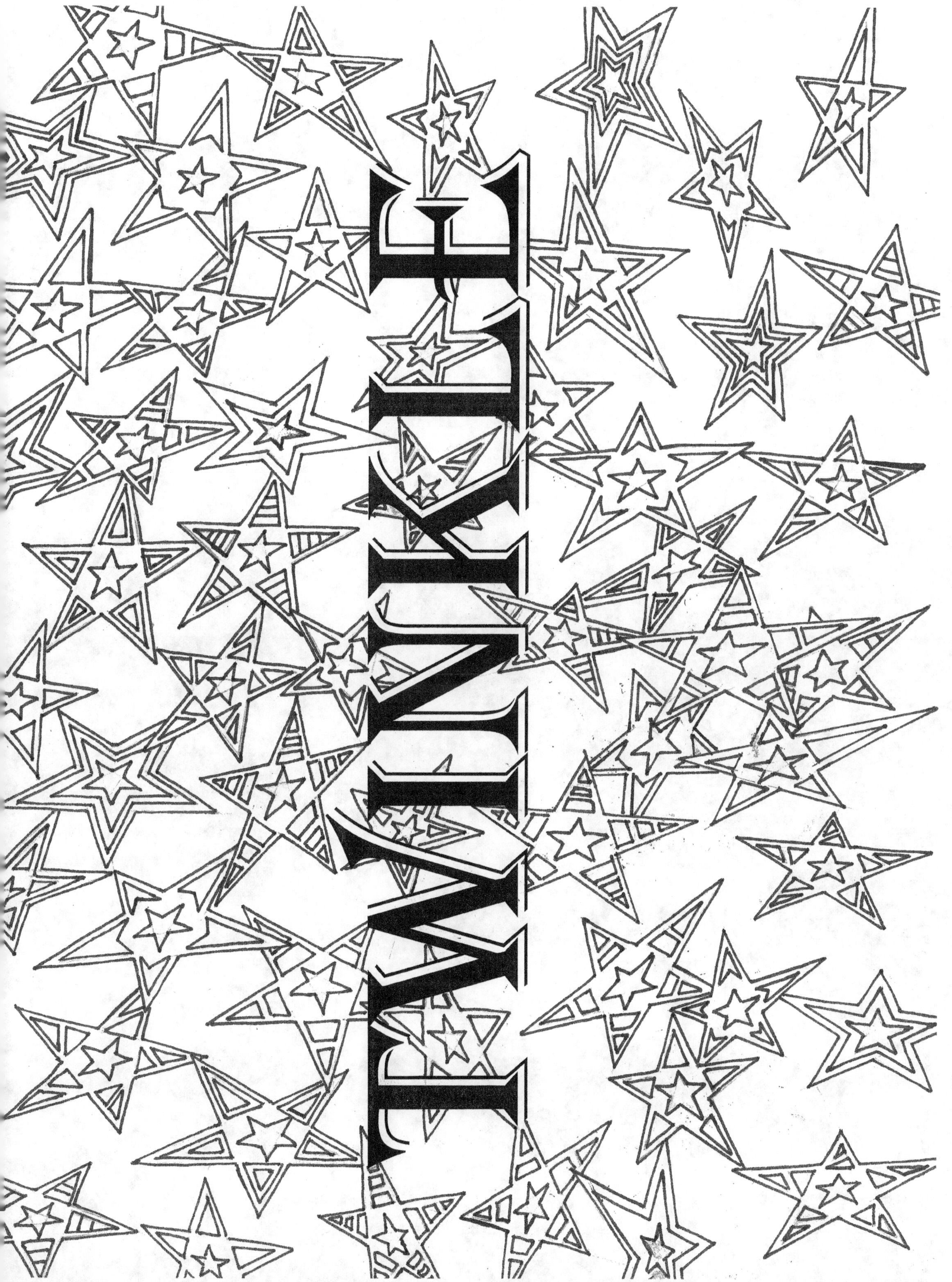
TWINKLE

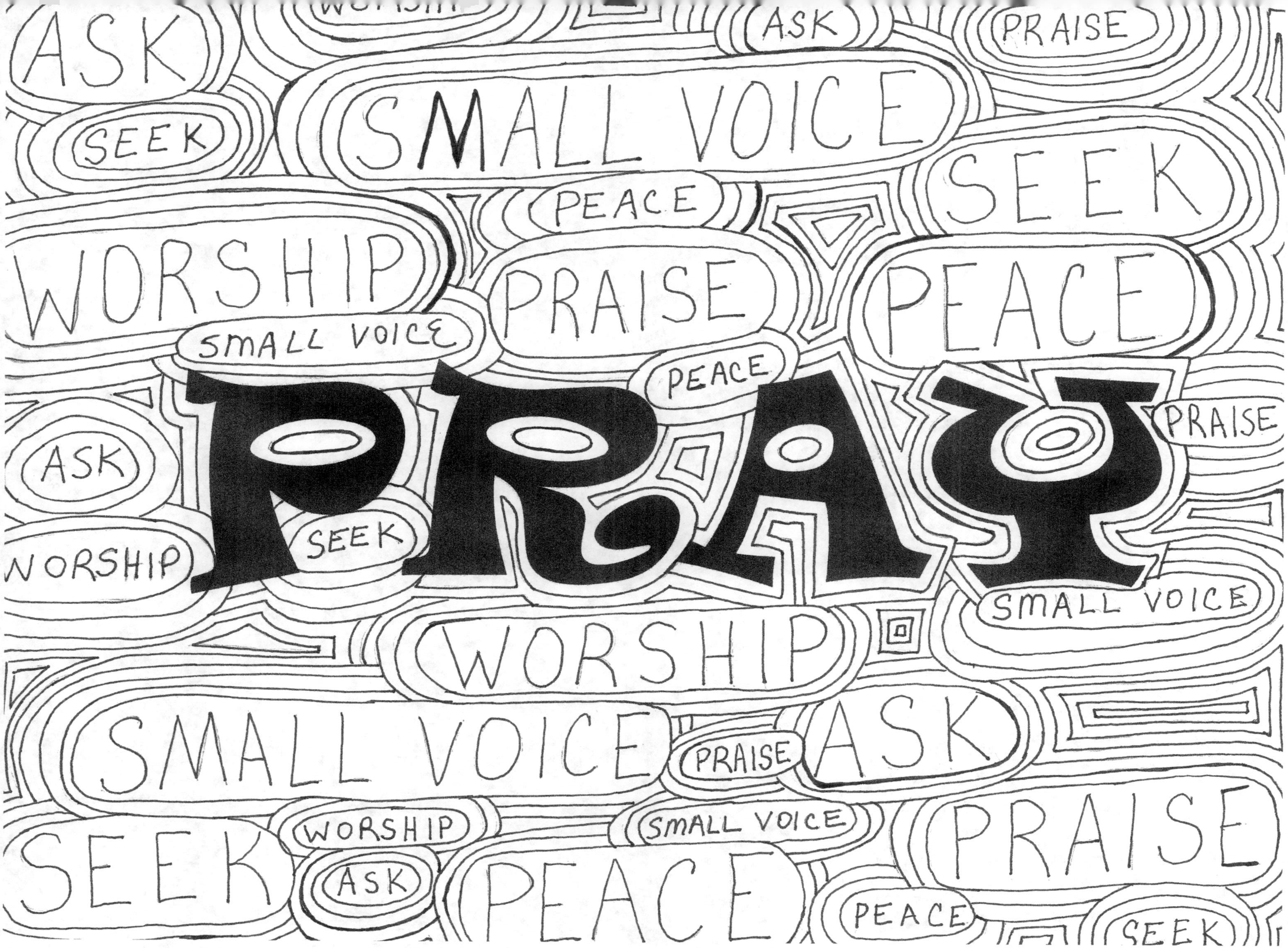
PRAY
ASK
ASK
PRAISE
SEEK
SMALL VOICE
SEEK
PEACE
WORSHIP
PRAISE
PEACE
SMALL VOICE
PEACE
PRAISE
ASK
SEEK
WORSHIP
SMALL VOICE
WORSHIP
SMALL VOICE
PRAISE
ASK
WORSHIP
SMALL VOICE
PRAISE
SEEK
ASK
PEACE
PEACE
SEEK

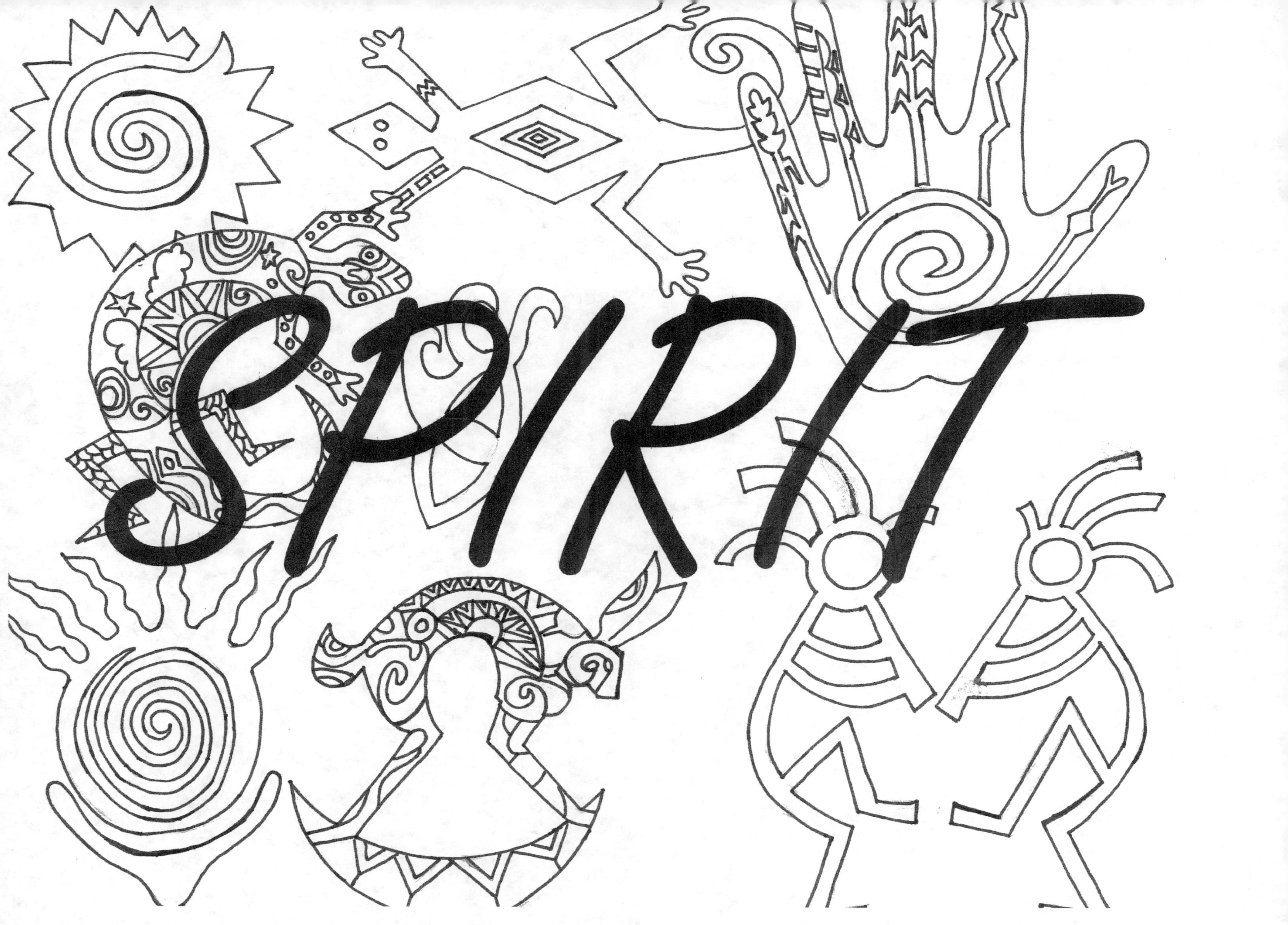
SPIRIT

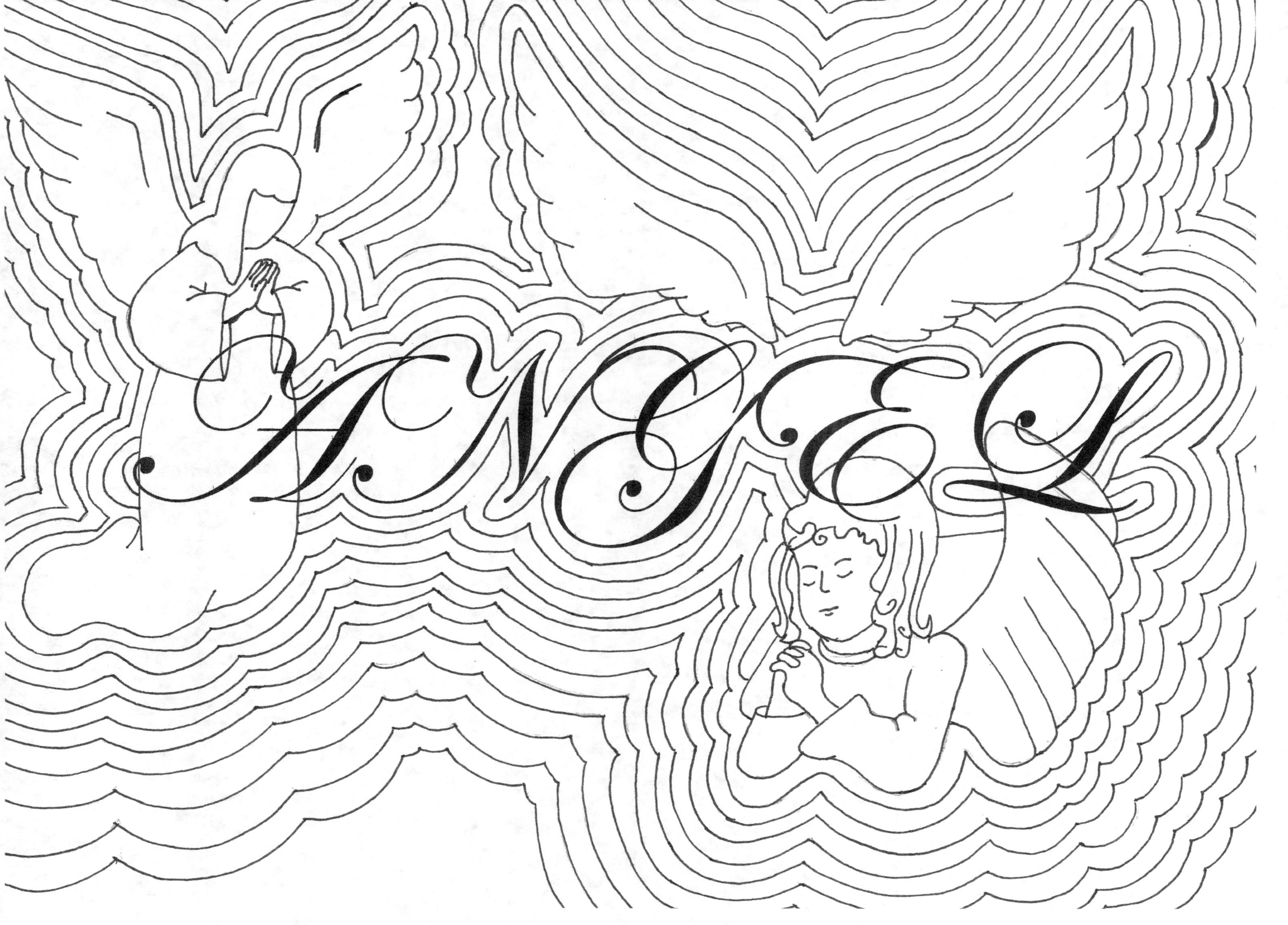
ANGEL

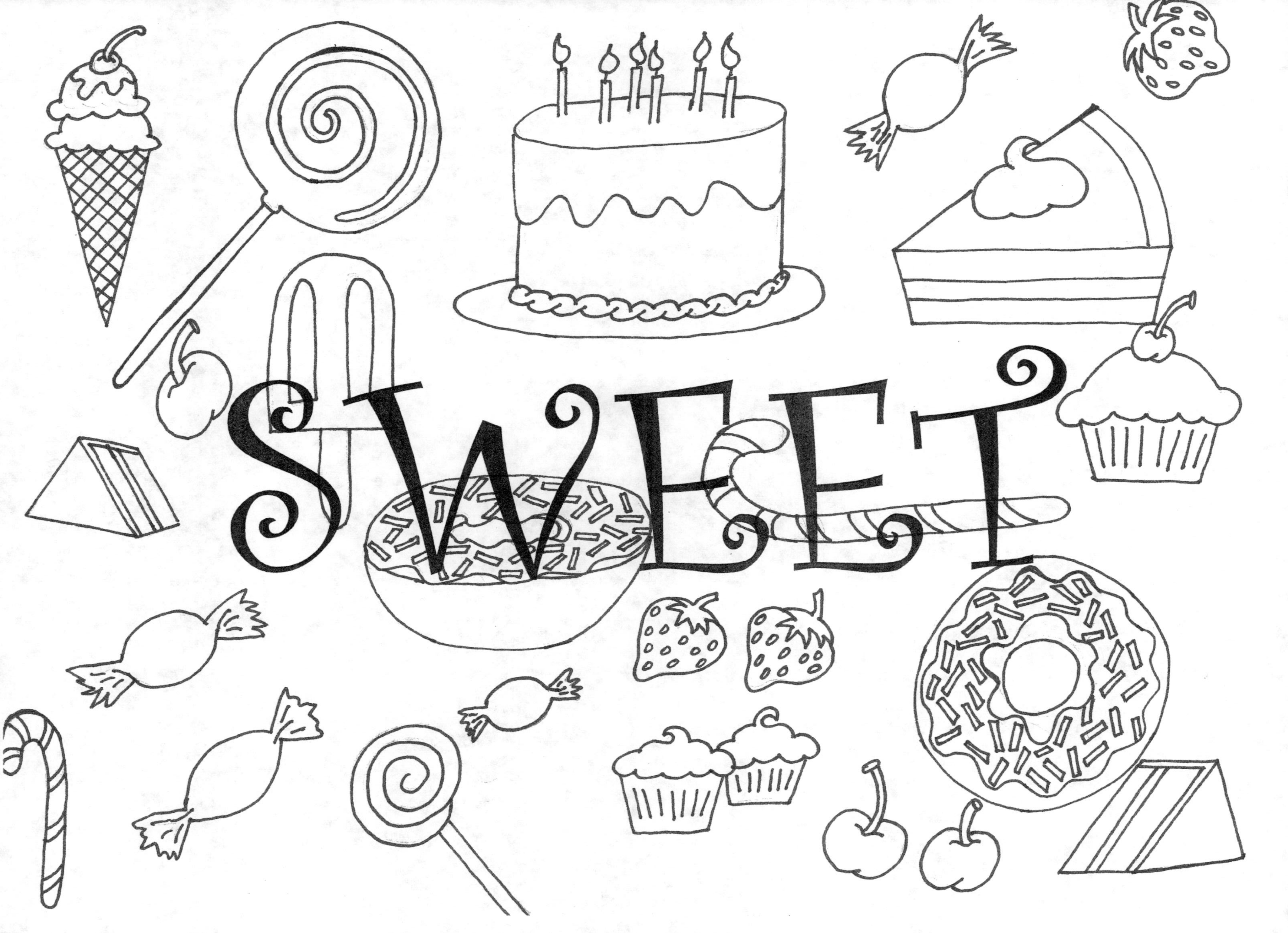
SWEET

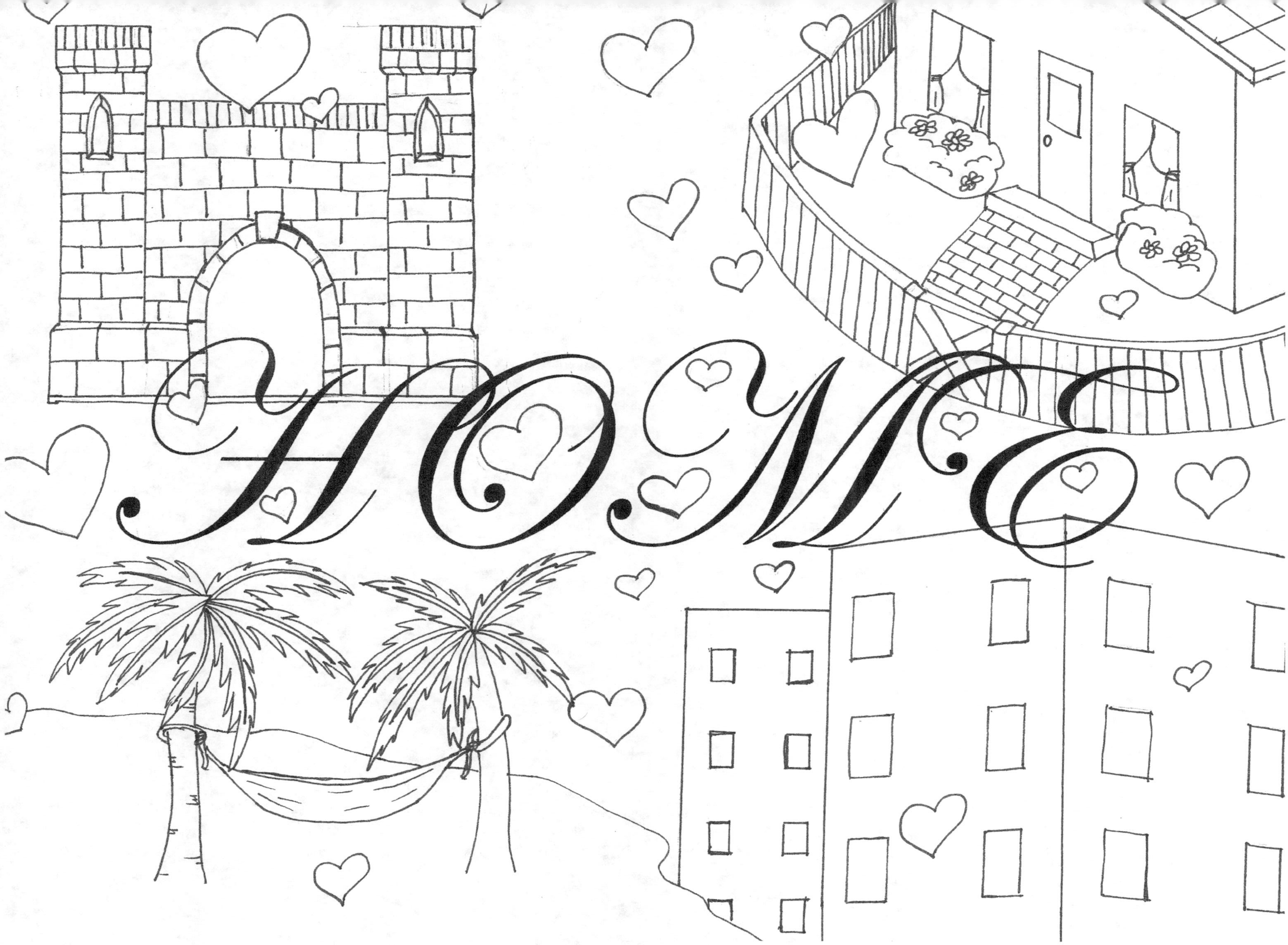
HOME

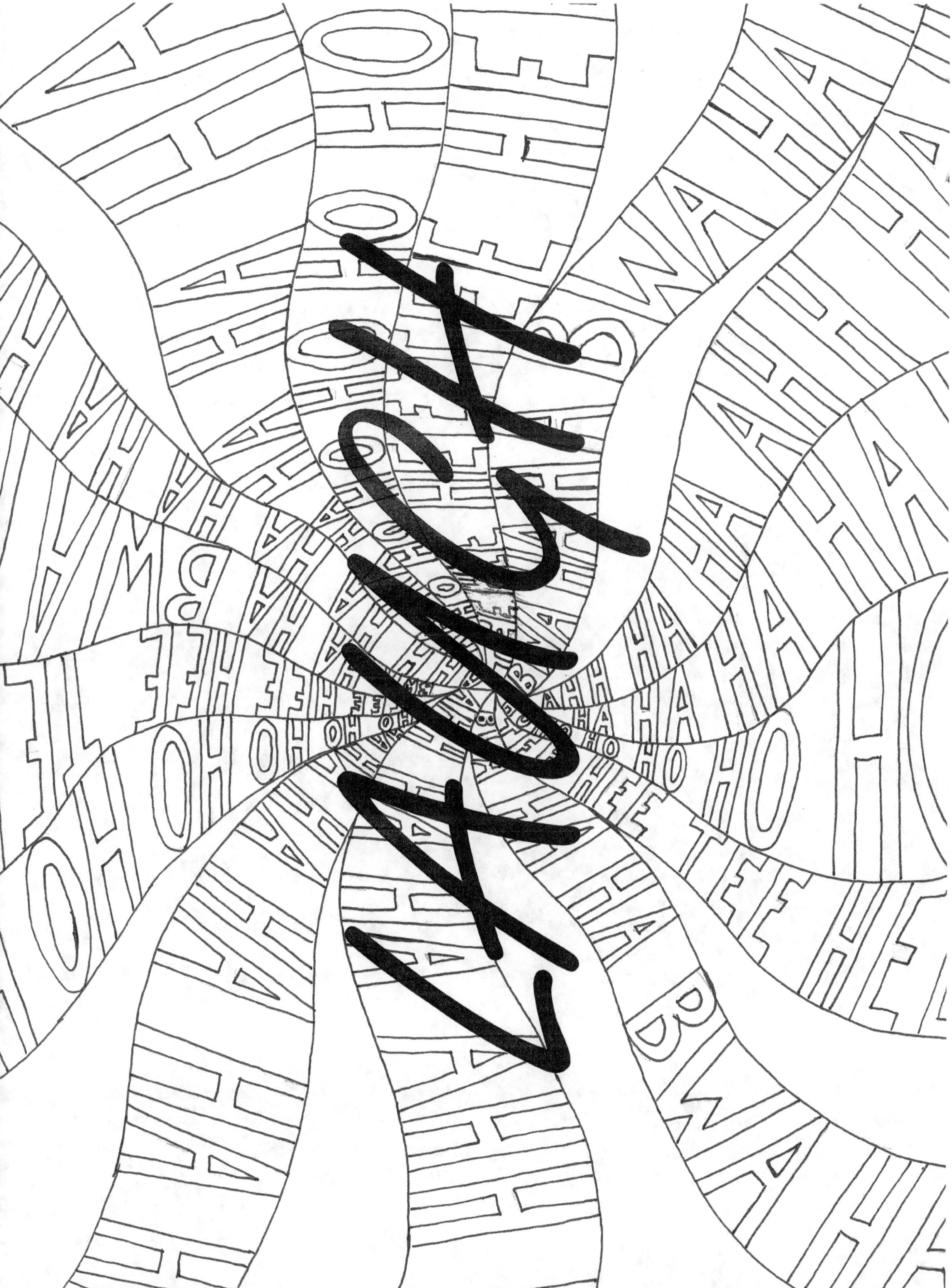
LAUGH

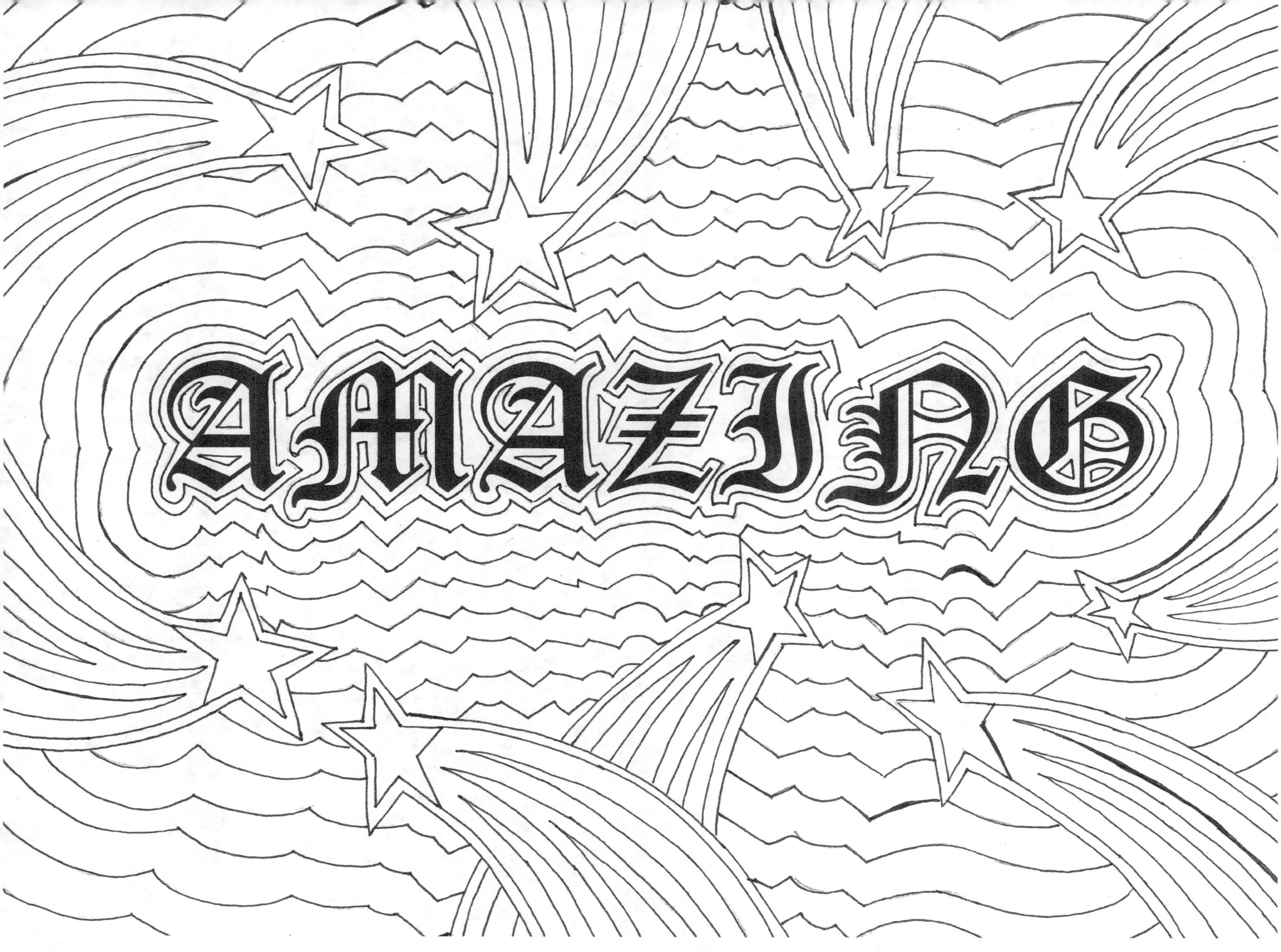
AMAZING

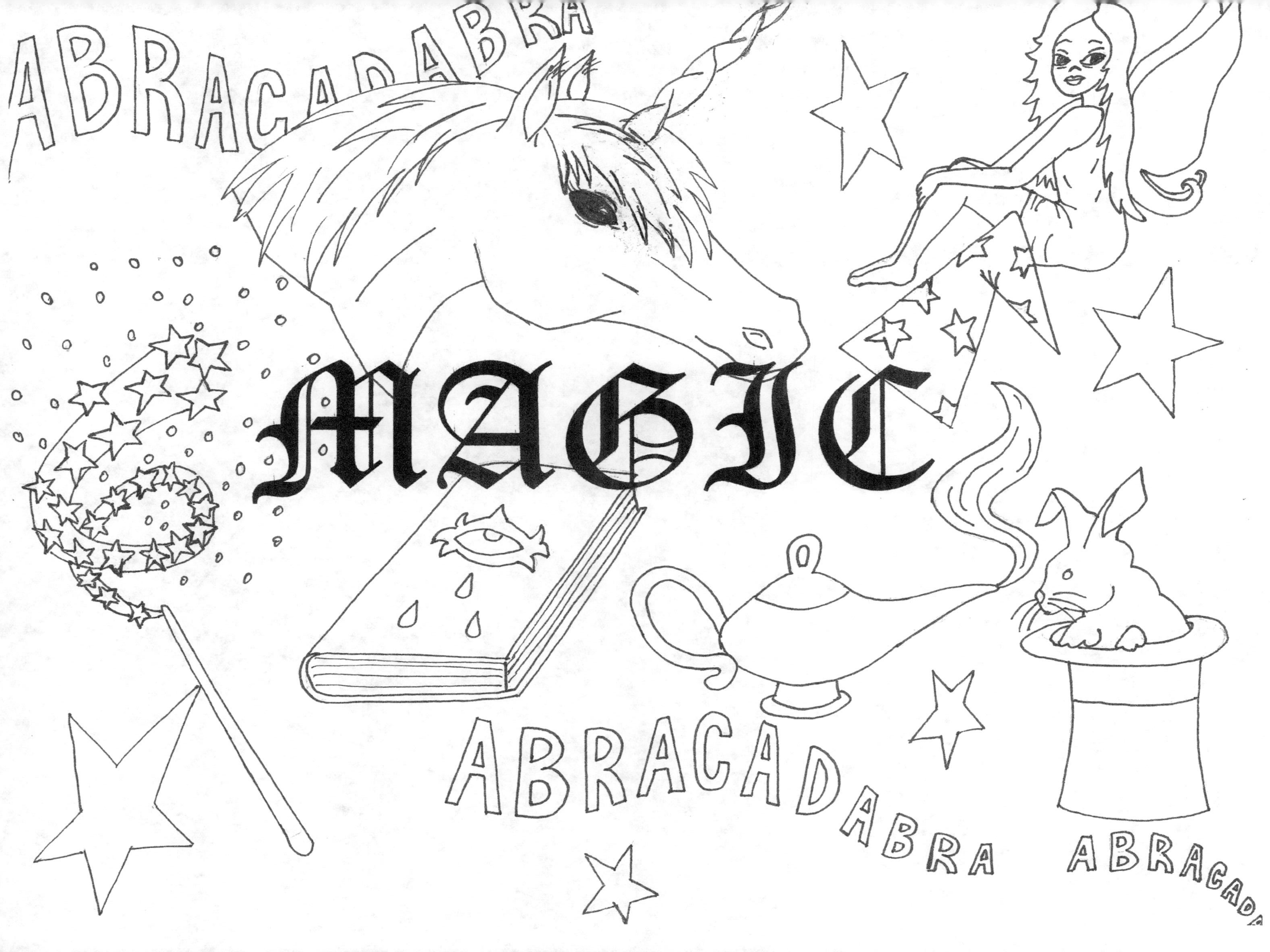
ABRACADABRA
MAGIC
ABRACADABRA
ABRACADA

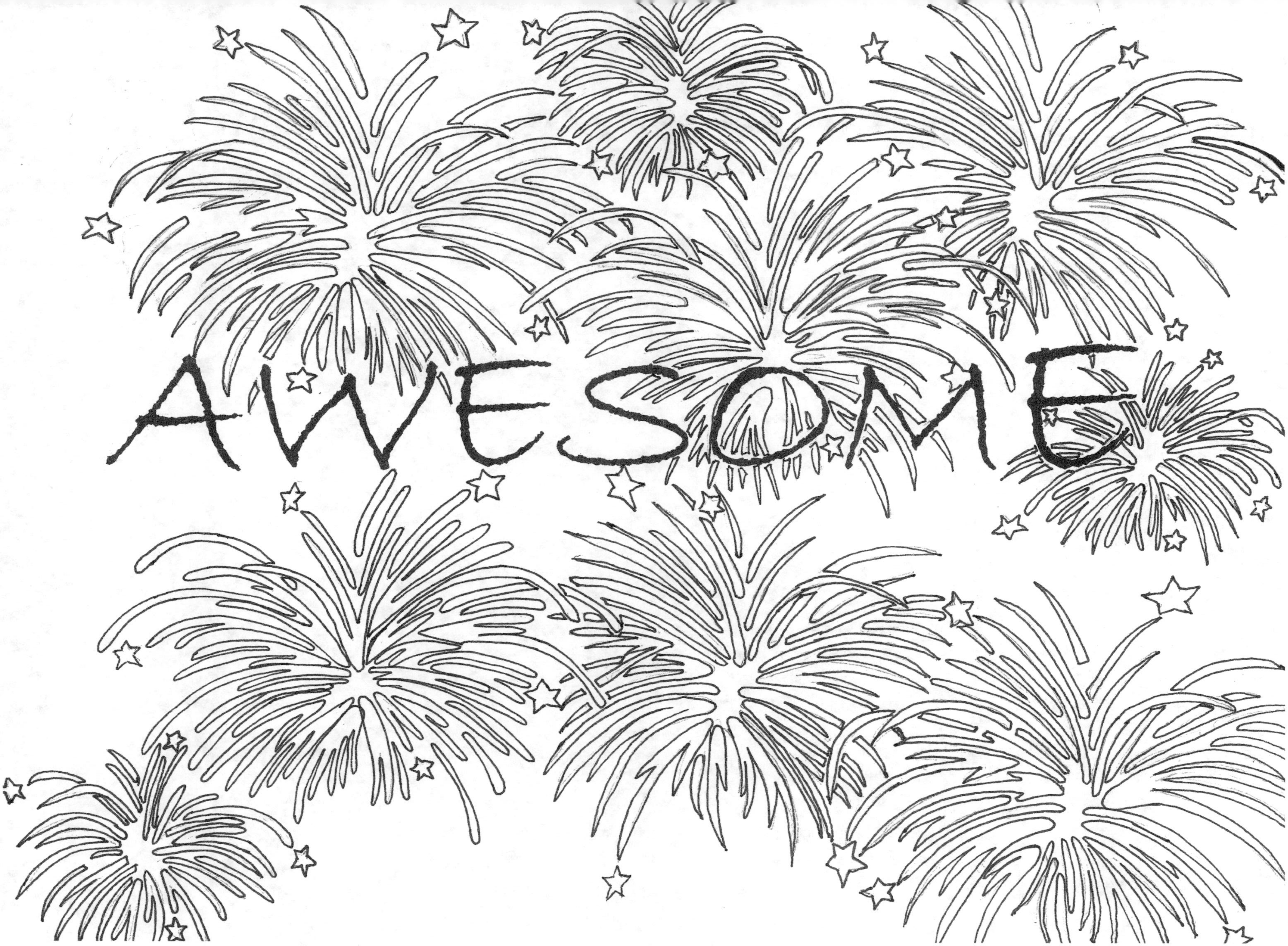
AWESOME

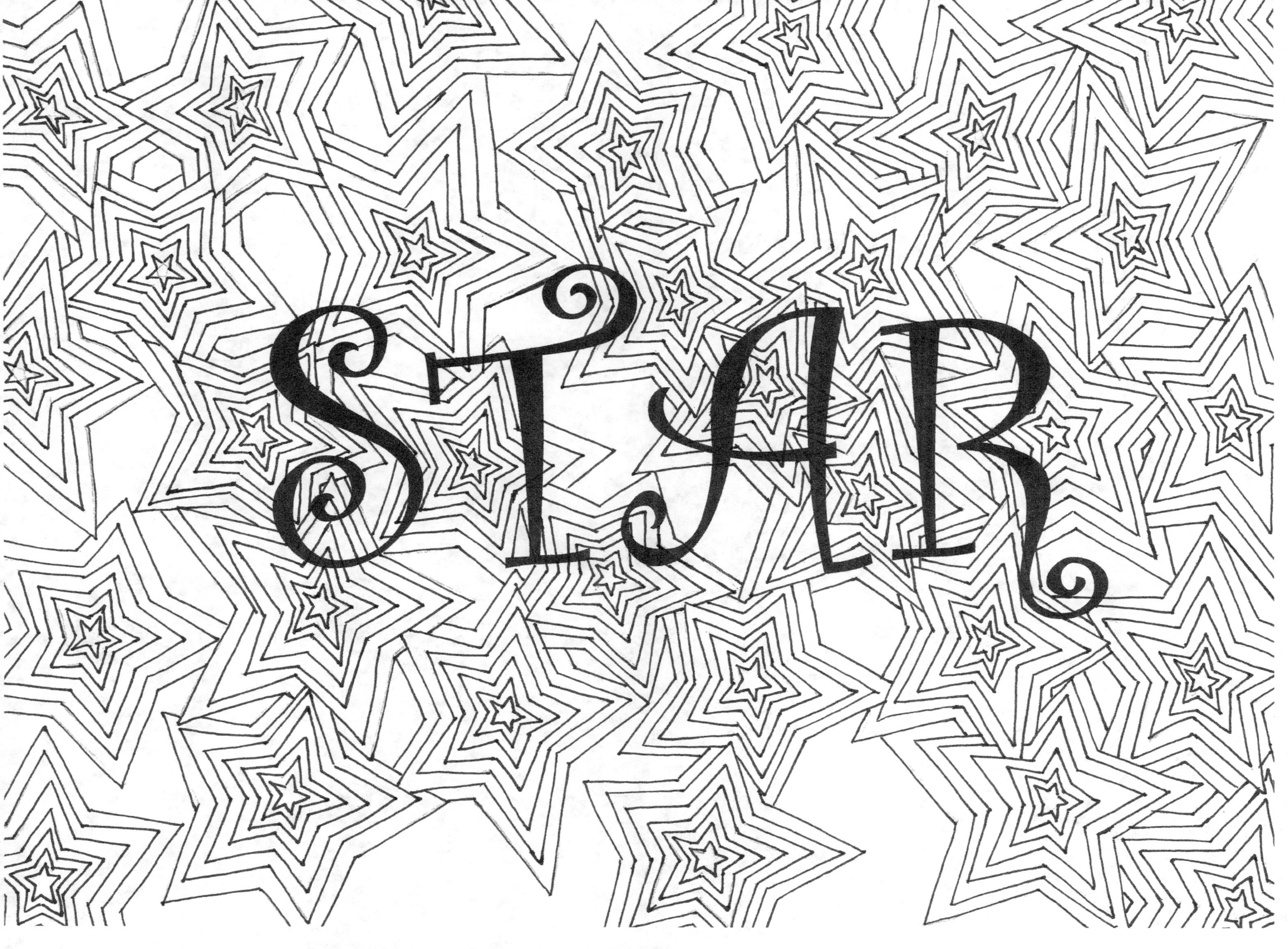
STAR

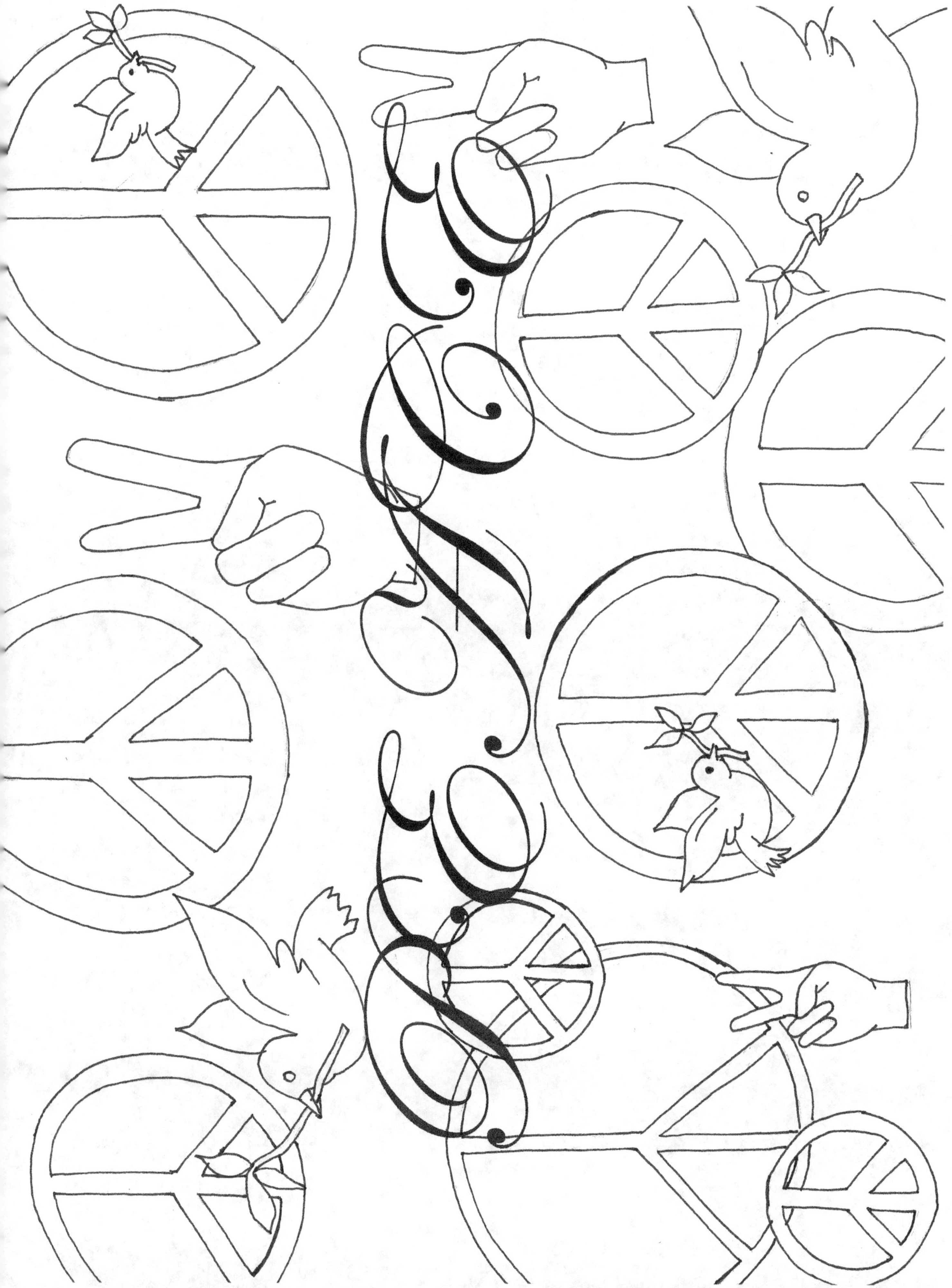
Peace

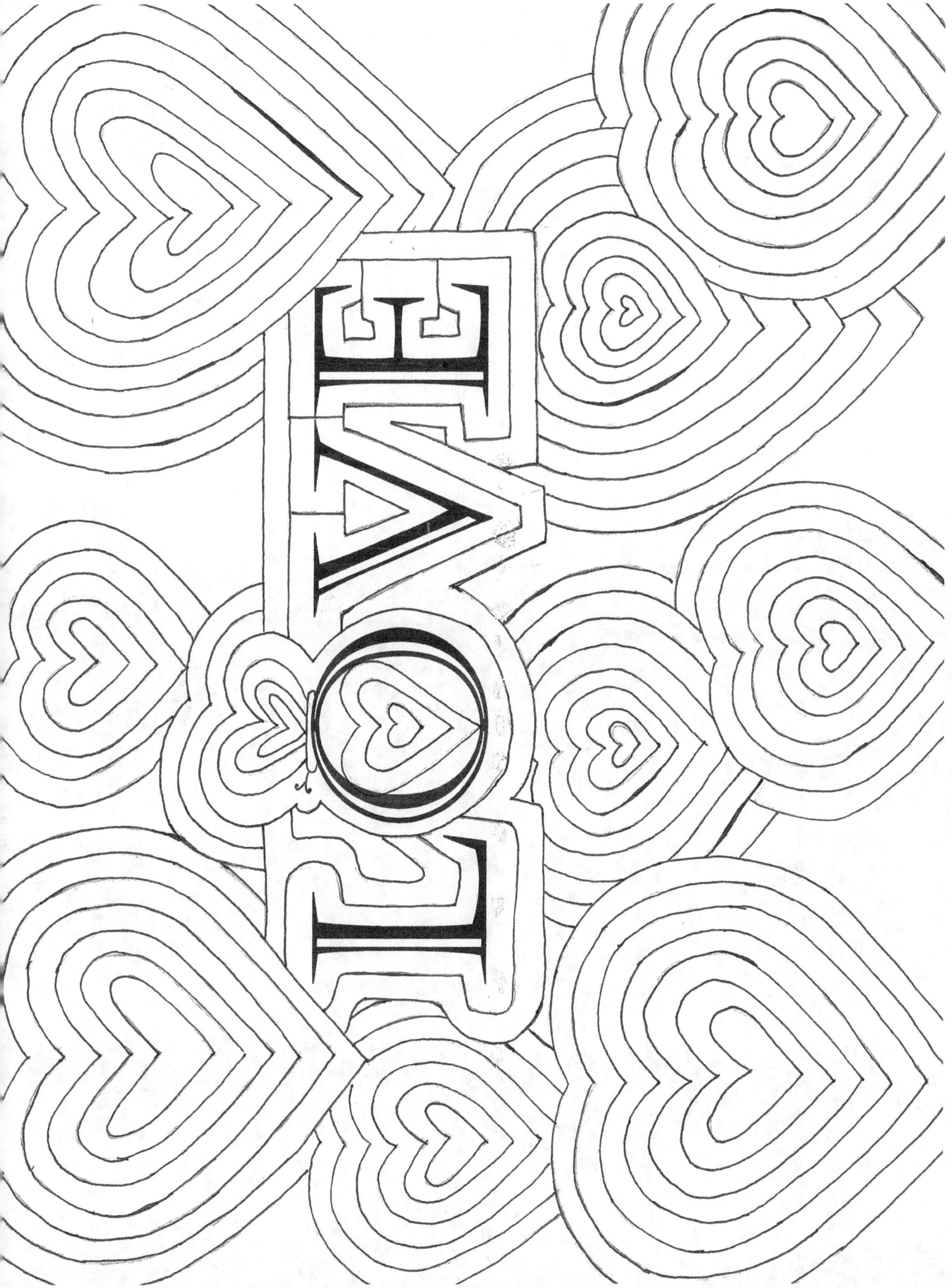
LOVE

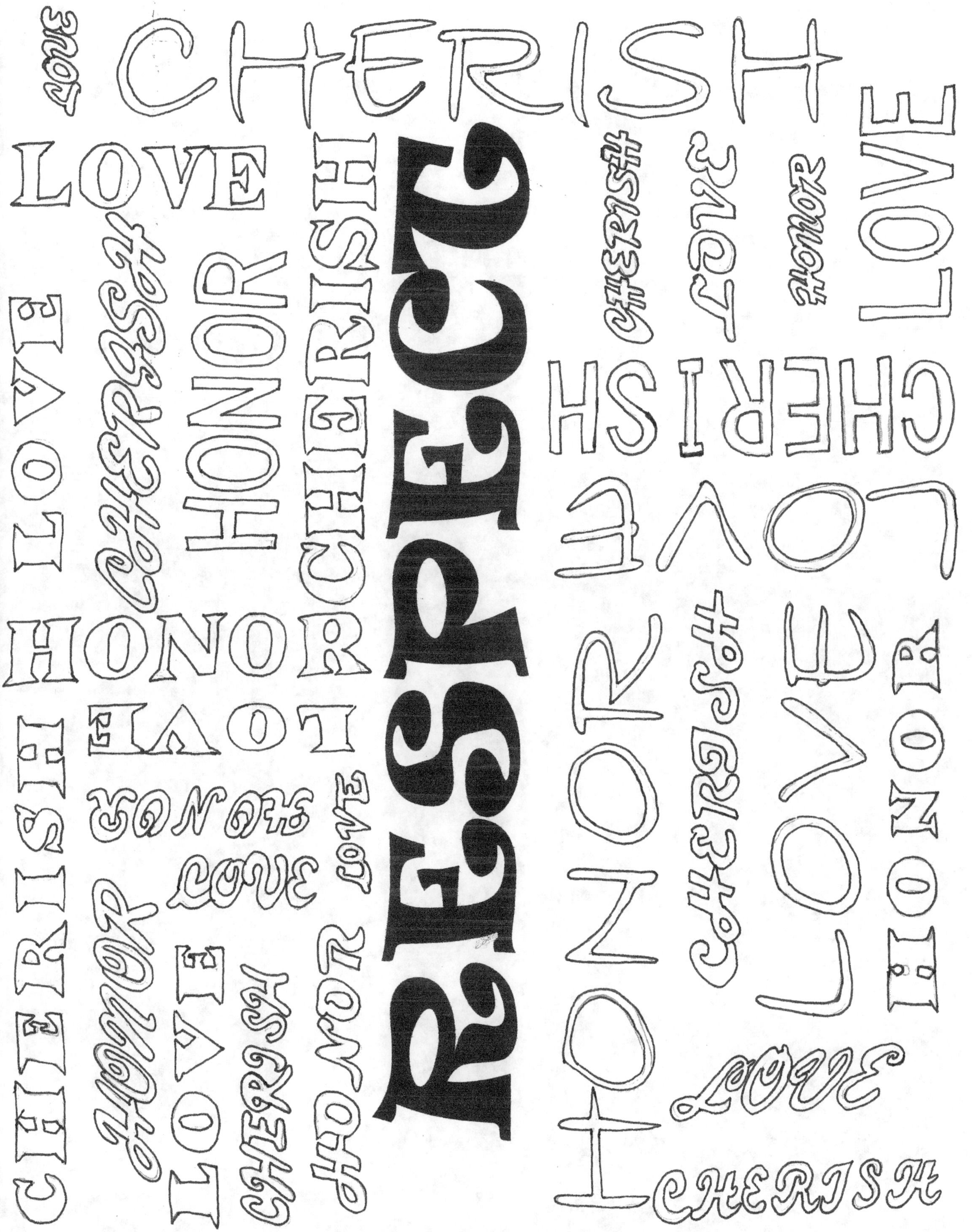
RESPECT
CHERISH
LOVE
HONOR
LOVE
CHERISH
HONOR
LOVE
CHERISH
LOVE
HONOR
CHERISH
LOVE
HONOR
LOVE
CHERISH

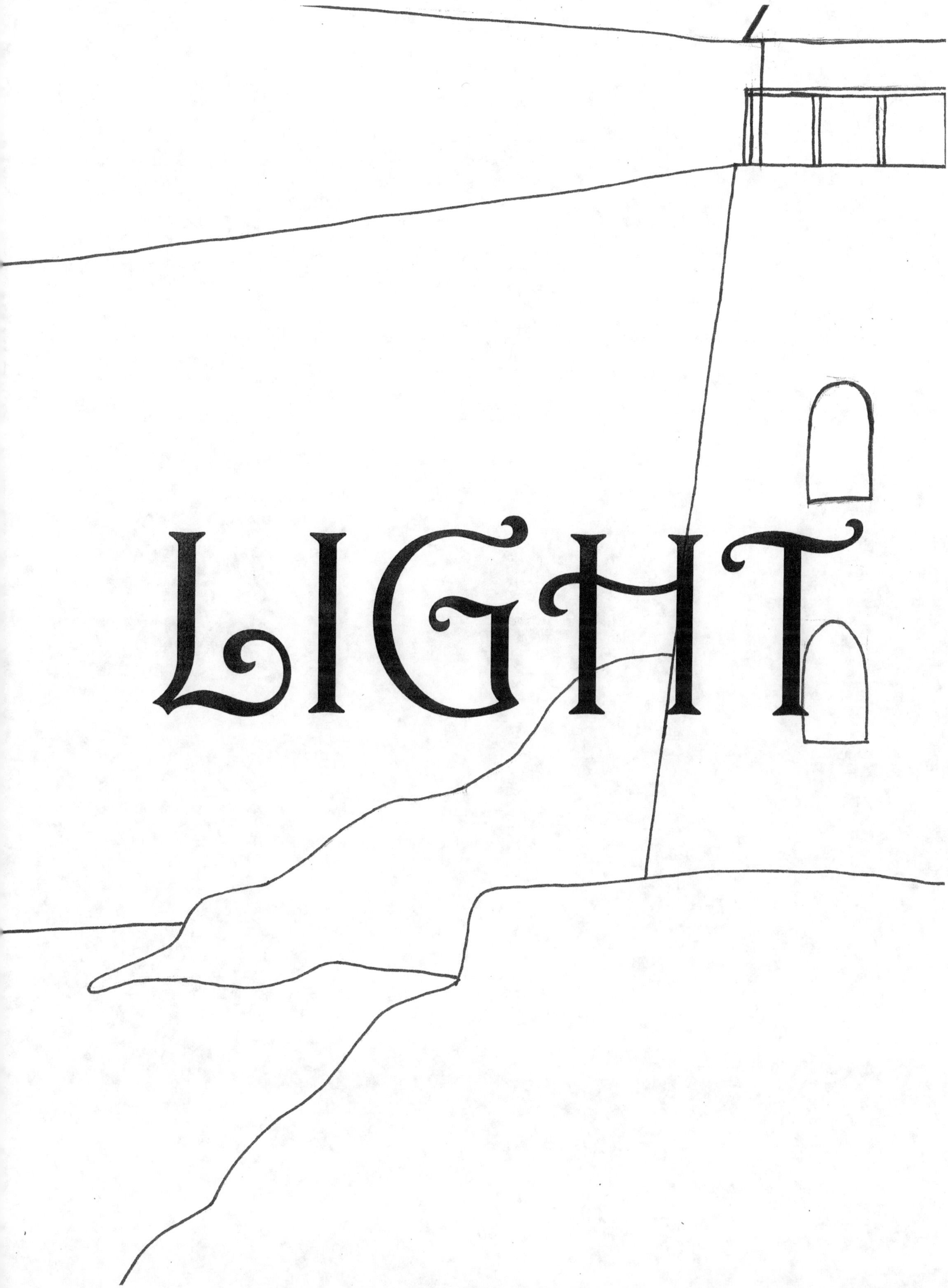
LIGHT

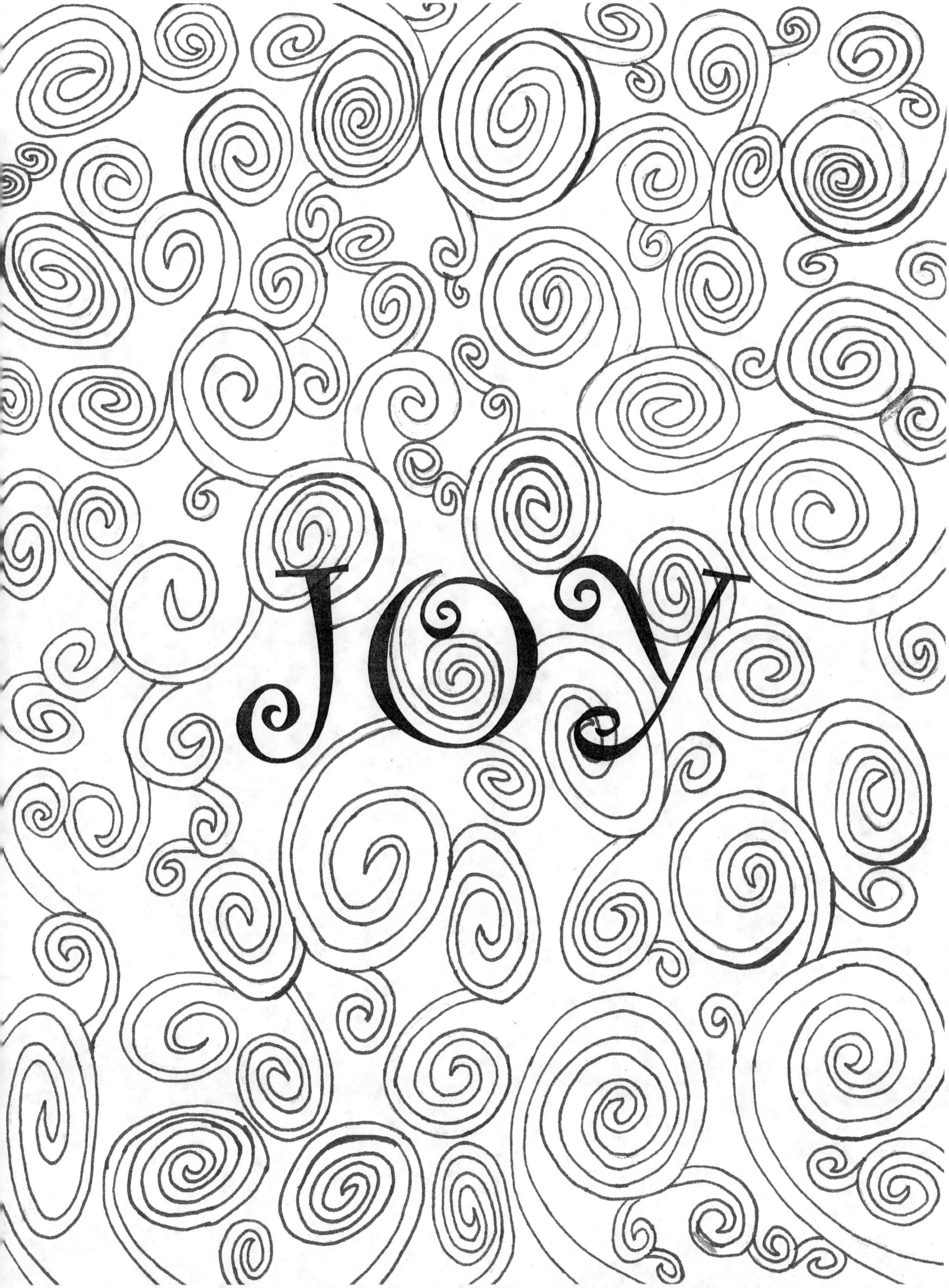
JOY

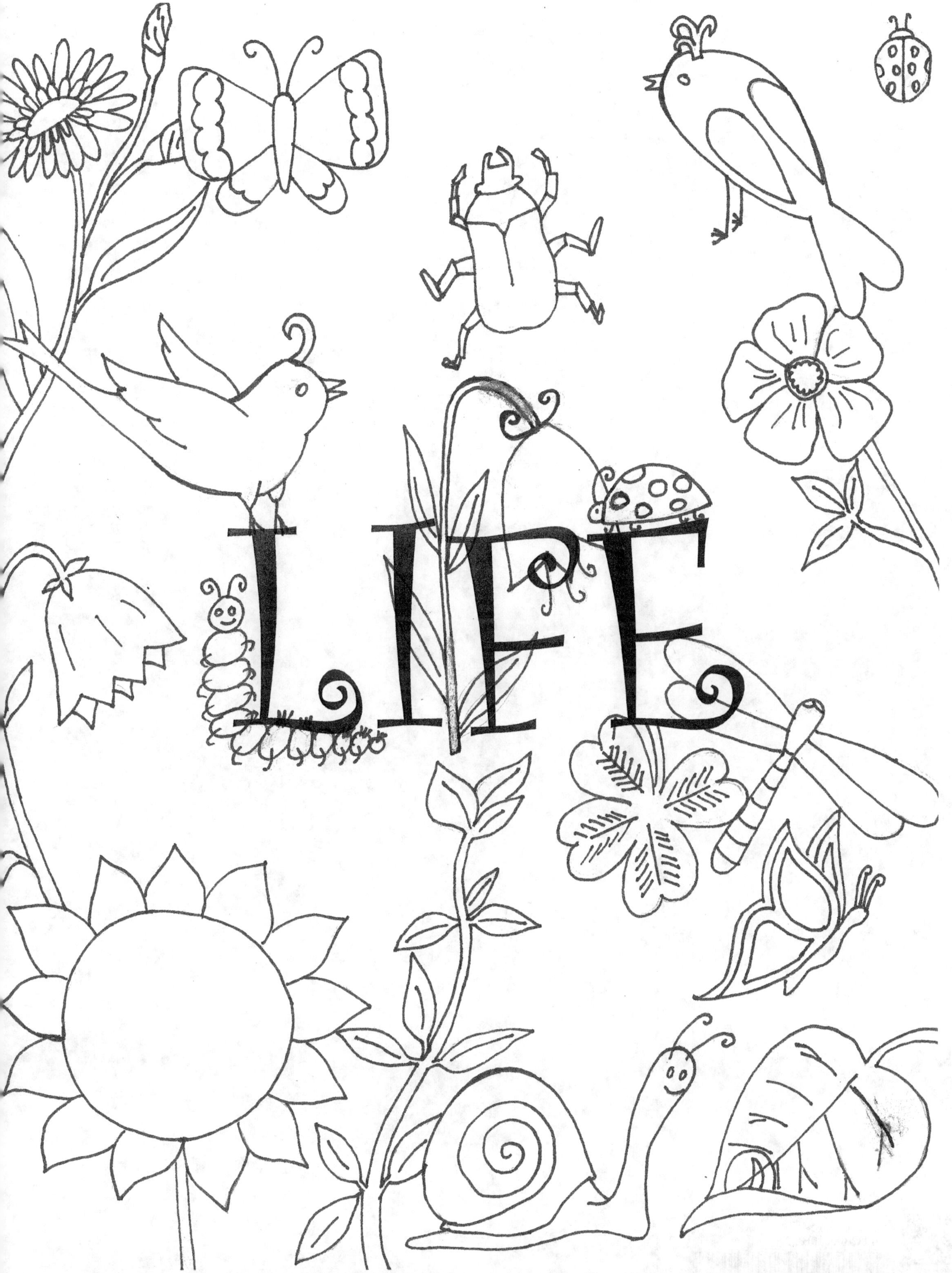
LIFE

www.ingramcontent.com/pod-product-compliance
Lightning Source LLC
Chambersburg PA
CBHW081617220526
45468CB00010B/2924
9781942761754